RETHINKING FANDOM

CRAIG CALCATERRA

RETHINKING FANDOM

FANDOM

How to Beat the Sports-Industrial Complex at Its Own Game

Belt Publishing

Printed in the United States of America
First edition 2022
1 2 3 4 5 6 7 8 9

ISBN: 978-1-953368-23-2

Belt Publishing
5322 Fleet Avenue
Cleveland, Ohio 44105
www.beltpublishing.com

Cover art by David Wilson
Book design by Meredith Pangrace

For the people in the cheap seats who give far more than they get.

CONTENTS

INTRODUCTION

In early 2019, Geoff Baker, an investigative sports reporter for the *Seattle Times* whose work I admire, was given a new responsibility by the paper: he was assigned to cover the new National Hockey League expansion team in Seattle. The team did not yet have a name and certainly did not have any players. Indeed, it was still nearly 1,000 days before the team would even begin play. Despite that, there was obviously a lot to cover. News about the future team's ownership group. News about the massive ongoing renovation to Seattle's arena, which would eventually be the team's home. News about the various rules and financial considerations that would directly impact the stocking of the team's roster and its competitive future in the NHL. Getting an expansion team going is pretty complicated, so it makes perfect sense that a major newspaper like the *Times* would dedicate someone to covering that beat.

But Baker's coverage also included something else: a weekly feature in which he responded to fan letters and emails. A great many fans had questions about those nuts-and-bolts issues on which Baker was reporting, of course, but there were often digressions by both the letter writer and Baker that revealed significant fan excitement around the new team. There was talk about the possibility of superfan groups like the Seattle Seahawks' famous "Twelfth Man."

I don't follow hockey very closely, and I have little interest in Seattle's sports, but whenever I'd see Baker tweet out links to his mailbag, I was fascinated with the idea that a nameless, faceless team could have actual fans already, let alone budding superfans. By the time the team was finally dubbed the Seattle Kraken and given a logo and colors in the summer of 2020, there had already been a year's worth of fan letters and emails crossing Baker's desk.

Upon even a little reflection, that's not terribly surprising. Fandom—be it about sports, movies, comic books, TV shows, video games, or almost anything else—is about more than the basic activity that inspires it. Most sports fans don't spend a ton of time examining *why* we're sports fans. Most of us haven't run cost-benefit analyses of being a sports fan as opposed to, say, getting into needlepoint or birdwatching. Sports are just something we like. Watching sports is just something we do. Being a sports fan is just something we are.

At root, fandom is about community and belonging. Bonding, even. It's about watching the games and the movies and reading the books, yes, but it's also about talking about them, even hypothetically. It's about forming connections and forging a tribe of people with similar interests. When those people with similar interests come from disparate backgrounds, it can create an all-too-rare convergence of people who may otherwise never interact, and that's a very good thing.

There can be negatives to fandom, as anything driven by passion can be taken to negative extremes. The term "fan" itself likely comes from this sort of unhealthy connotation. Though the word's origins are a little murky, etymologists tend to credit the nineteenth-century baseball manager and scout Ted Sullivan for the term's origin. Sullivan said in the 1890s that "fan" was short for "fanatic," putting it in league with the terms "crank" and "bug." Whether sports fandom brings positives or negatives, though, it is hard to escape the notion that sports fandom is, to a very large degree, driven by a certain irrationality and is often an emotional exercise.

Fandom and, more specifically, identification with a particular team, tends to be inherited. To the extent that psychologists have studied sports fandom—a very,

very small field of study, it should be noted—they have discovered, perhaps not surprisingly, that a majority of sports fans, usually around 60 percent, say that their introduction to sports came via a family member, more often than not through a father or father figure. For this reason, fandom is best thought of as an identity as opposed to an allegiance asserted by conscious choice. An identity that is bolstered by friendships, social encouragement, geography, and personal and cultural inertia. Watching games, following sports news, and finding a place in our minds and in our hearts for all that surrounds sports is just a thing we do because, for the most part, we've always done it, not because we're making objective decisions on the matter.

In a 2018 study, researchers found that fans of sports teams and supporters of political parties perceive news in much the same way, with fans viewing news stories accusing their team of wrongdoing—such as the violation of rules or engaging in sharp dealings—as biased regardless of the substance of the report. This operated in much the same way, researchers concluded, as reactions political partisans had to stories about their party in media outlets perceived to be hostile to their interests. They concluded that sports fans, like political partisans, filtered new information through the lens of group affiliation, relying on it as a mental shortcut to help make decisions. Once sports fandom had become a part of their identity, using their group identification to make judgments when faced with controversies became a powerful motivator. It often caused fans to interpret objective criticism of their favorite teams as a personal attack or to assume the mindset that their interests and the interests of the teams they root for are aligned when they really are not.

This book is about that place—the place where a fan's interests and a team's interests diverge. It is about how sports teams and leagues, often in concert with political actors, the media, and business interests, which I collectively consider to be a kind of "sports-industrial complex," can and do use our often irrational devotion and loyalty for their own purposes, and actively hurting the teams we love, the cities we call home, the athletes we can't stop watching. Sometimes, they even hinder the progress of social justice. This book is about how to identify those moments when the sports-industrial complex is working against our interests and what, if anything, we can do about it.

In politics, we've increasingly seen the idea that the scoreboard is all that matters. Winning elections is the ultimate objective for candidates as opposed to a means to the end of policy and the shaping of society. We've likewise increasingly seen the notion that "our team" and "the opposing team" is the proper way to view the parties to the relevant contest. These concepts, which make sense to varying degrees in the context of sports, have been imported into politics and have served to degrade them.

At the same time, sports fans and commentators have eagerly begun to traffic in political-style reality creation, distortion, and spin. Bomb-throwing and pot-stirring "hot takers" like Fox Sports's Skip Bayless arguably have more influence over sports discourse than respected experts who depend on rational analysis to make their points, aping the way in which political discourse has become more a creature of cable news partisans than of Sunday magazine shows or weekly newspaper editorials. Not terribly long ago, one of the largest sports media outlets, Vox Media's SB Nation, would routinely remind its writers that "sports are tribal," and would strongly encourage them to write in a way that reinforced rooting interests and rivalries among fan bases, much in the way a partisan talk show host or cable news anchor may lean into their audience's biases.

None of this is to say, of course, that sports fandom is necessarily toxic. This book is not meant to disparage your fandom on the basis of its inherent irrationality. I'm a sports fan too, after all, and even if sports fandom is an often irrational exercise, it is an eminently understandable one. The research of sports fandom—how it informs and interacts with a person's identity, how it affects their behavior, and how it causes fans to process information—is a relatively new pursuit, but so far there has been little correlation found between one's identifying strongly as a fan of a given team and one's propensity to act violently or antisocially in the name of that fandom. Indeed, sports fans who have been found to highly identify themselves with a given team tend to exhibit higher levels of self-esteem, an increased tendency toward positive emotions, and a decreased tendency toward negative emotions in their life overall. Being a sports fan is associated with lower levels of depression and alienation and higher levels of belonging and self-worth. Sports fandom has likewise been found to provide individual fans with coping strategies in the face of setbacks and a greater sense of optimism in the face of challenges.

This book will not tell you to give up sports or to turn your back on the team you love. Yes, there *are* a lot of bad things about sports. Personally, I quit watching pro football many years ago because I could not abide the way in which the sport breaks people's bodies and minds. I also quit watching all college sports because I could not, in good conscience, be a part of the inherent exploitation of unpaid labor for the enrichment of the sports-industrial complex. Those, however, were personal decisions, and I don't presume to have a monopoly on wisdom when it comes to such things, let alone the authority to tell you what to do. Either way, if you're to the point where your displeasure with that which surrounds a given sport or sports in general is so great that you are seriously questioning whether you should even continue to watch them, you don't need anyone's help to push you that extra inch. Certainly not an entire book's worth of help.

But like I said: giving up your sports fandom is not what this book is about. I'm interested in trying to find a way to hold on to that which we love about sports while not being used or taken advantage of by a sports-industrial complex that wants to leverage our loyalty for its own purposes. As is the case with anything else that serves those ends, be it family, politics, religion, or social bonds of other forms, sports fandom is capable of being exploited by the people who disingenuously cast sports teams as institutions with an outsized role in the health of a city, thereby entitling them to the sorts of privileges and protections normal businesses don't get. Or the people who try to leverage your civic pride, as filtered through the triumphs of a local team, as a means of covering up problems in society. The people who work hard to extract money from your pocket and from public treasuries for shiny, expensive new sports stadiums, which will allegedly be a public good, but which in reality turn out to be playgrounds for the wealthy. The people who claim that those new stadiums are necessary to build a winning team but who then proceed in a way that makes clear that profits, not championships, are their top priority. The people who venerate the athletes when they are hitting home runs, scoring touchdowns, or putting up triple-doubles but who seek to break them at the bargaining table and engage in anti-labor practices when they demand to be paid fairly for their services. The people who are complicit in advancing a harmful and retrograde social and political agenda and who, when anyone questions it, casts those people as disloyal or unpatriotic.

In the first part of the book, I will focus on specific instances in which the sports-industrial complex counts on your loyalty, your devotion, and passion and then leverages that loyalty, devotion, and passion to its advantage and, quite often, to your detriment or the detriment of the community in which you live. Instances in which the sports-industrial complex takes your fandom for granted and assumes that because you rooted for a team and supported it when you were young, you will continue to do so forever. Instances in which you are made to choose between your support of a team and your support of the athletes who play for it. Instances in which you are made to choose between what is best for your community and what is best for your rooting interest. Instances in which you are made to feel that if you question or criticize what the sports-industrial complex does, you are committing some sort of transgression, not just against the team, but even against the country.

In the second part, I will offer specific approaches to sports that allow you to continue to partake in the enjoyable aspects of sports fandom while minimizing the negatives and not allowing yourself to be used and manipulated by the sports-industrial complex.

We may feel powerless at the hands of the sports-industrial complex. They run the show. They own the teams. They employ the players. They are the keepers of the history, the colors, the uniforms, and the lore that are inextricably tied up in our love of sports and our fandom for a particular team. But we're not powerless. We may not be able to *stop* them from wanting to engage in the worst sorts of behavior, but we can make it so that when they do, we are not being taken along for the ride. We can do this by examining the way in which we relate to sports. By attempting to discover different ways to relate to sports. By, on a very fundamental level, rethinking our fandom.

PART I

THE STATE OF
MODERN FANDOM

1
ROOTING FOR LAUNDRY

I became an Atlanta Braves fan in 1985. At the time, the team's big star was outfielder Dale Murphy. His supporting cast on the Braves was not particularly strong, but I liked many of them. The ones I remember most vividly were first baseman Bob Horner, shortstop Rafael Ramírez, pitcher Rick Mahler, third baseman Ken Oberkfell, second baseman Glenn Hubbard, and relief pitcher Gene Garber. They were all still with the team in 1986. In 1987, though, Horner left to go play in Japan, and Gene Garber was traded to Kansas City. In 1988, Ramírez was traded to Houston, Oberkfell was traded to Pittsburgh, and Hubbard left via free agency for Oakland. In 1989, Mahler signed as a free agent with the Cincinnati Reds. Finally, in 1990, the Braves traded Dale Murphy to the Philadelphia Phillies.

The Braves were a pretty terrible team between 1985 and 1990, finishing in last place in four of those six seasons and second to last in the other two. In 1991, though, they turned things around completely, going from worst to first, winning the National League pennant and falling one game shy of winning the World Series. I cheered my head off all year long. I cheered despite the fact that all of my favorite players from the time I had started rooting for the team had been shipped off or left. Indeed, none of the players from that 1985 Braves team were around for that 1991 pennant. The roster had completely turned over.

The Greek philosopher Plutarch wasn't a fan of the 1980s Atlanta Braves, but he caught the vibe of them, and every other professional sports team in the post-free agency era, with his thought exercise "the ship of Theseus." You may have heard this one before:

> The ship wherein Theseus and the youth of Athens returned had thirty oars, and was preserved by the Athenians down even to the time of Demetrius Phalereus, for they took away the old planks as they decayed, putting in new and stronger timber in their place, insomuch that this ship became a standing example among the philosophers, for the logical question of things that grow; one side holding that the ship remained the same, and the other contending that it was not the same.

At some point, all the boards in the ship must've been switched out, right? So, is it still the same ship? If not, at what point does it cease to be the ship of Theseus? Replacing one board is not a big deal, but what about when half of them are no longer original? What about most of them? What about when all of the boards had been pried out with crowbars and traded to the Phillies?

Various philosophers—also not baseball fans—have proposed solutions to this paradox over the centuries. None of them are particularly satisfying. Some have claimed that the ship was no longer itself once half the planks were replaced. Given that in my particular metaphor, the planks that were Atlanta Braves players didn't all leave at once, that seems arbitrary. Certainly in real time, in my childhood, I never felt, "Oh no, my Braves no longer exist!" After all, some of those replacement planks—Tom Glavine, John Smoltz, and David Justice— were pretty nice.

Other philosophers have claimed that no identity survives change. Under that scenario, the Atlanta Braves ceased being the team I loved the moment Bob Horner joined the Yakult Swallows of the Japanese Central League. That's patently ridiculous, though. Players get traded for and away all the time, and such an approach would require a complete reassessment of fandom every year. Often multiple times within a single year. Besides, Horner was getting out of shape and was past his prime by then. That board was going to have to be replaced soon anyway.

Another solution comes from Ludwig Wittgenstein, who bypassed all of the mental gymnastics and said that the name "ship of Theseus" can be applied to whatever we want. It's all relative, in other words, so the 1985 Braves, 1991 Braves, and 2022 Braves are all, for my purposes, the same thing. Happy cheering.

Wittgenstein's solution is how, I suspect, just about every sports fan approaches the problem of players coming and going and rosters overturning. The problem, though, is that by taking that approach, sports fandom essentially boils down to rooting for corporate trademarks, colors, and iconography. Or, as the famous Jerry Seinfeld bit went, "It's different guys every year. You're rooting for clothes, when you get right down to it. We're screaming about laundry."

At the time Seinfeld told that joke, free agency in baseball had only been around for fifteen years. Modern, unrestricted free agency in basketball and football was even newer than that. The idea of our beloved players picking up and leaving a team in the middle of their career was still novel and, on some level, sort of unsettling. It caused sports columnists to rail against greedy, disloyal athletes, and it led the wealthy owners of sports teams to claim, erroneously, that they'd be bankrupted if they were forced to pay their free agents to stay with the team where they began. Fans, for the most part, bought into those notions. They increasingly began to view players less as the heroes of their youth or of bygone eras but as something more akin to mercenaries. As the players began to come and go, fans' attachment to the team—the replacement version of Theseus's ship, the trademarks, the laundry—became stronger.

There is at least something of a psychological basis for rooting for your team's trademarks and uniforms (or laundry, if you will). That sort of fandom, as noted before, was more likely than not something inherited. A fandom which allows you to be part of an in-group, often locally based, with the trappings of civic pride making up for the players who come and go. It's a step removed from the action on the field, on the court, or on the ice—separate and apart from the visceral and aesthetic aspects of watching sports—but it makes a certain amount of sense given the tribal nature of sports fandom.

But there are other modes of fandom, which have become increasingly prevalent in recent years, that seem even more disconnected from the sorts of psychological impulses and incentives that traditionally motivate sports fans.

In baseball, the field of advanced statistical analysis, or sabermetrics, became widely known by virtue of Michael Lewis's 2003 bestseller *Moneyball* and the subsequent film of the same name. Sabermetrics and other statistical studies of baseball had been around a long time, but when Lewis's book came out, it was still pretty novel for an actual baseball team's front office to employ them. That dramatically changed in the early 2000s, and in turn, the way baseball players are assessed and valued by teams changed dramatically as well.

In its original conception, sabermetrically minded baseball executives were cast as Davids to the Goliaths that comprised the baseball establishment, thinking outside the box to take advantage of inefficiencies in player assessment in order to sign good, useful but overlooked players and build competitive teams on the cheap. That David vs. Goliath dynamic appealed to a great many fans, particularly those who were conversant in statistical analysis and who were thus able to make the same sorts of assessments of players and teams using sabermetric concepts, granting them insight and expertise into the way baseball teams are run that older methods such as relying on one's authority as a "baseball man" with years of experience in the game did not. This, in turn, led to a veneration of baseball executives who proved themselves to be sabermetrically savvy and smarter than the others. In all ways that mattered, this constituted rooting for executives. Rooting for them against other executives, yes, but also against the players with whom they were negotiating contracts. Sabermetric message boards were filled with praise for front office executives who excelled at putting together winning teams with low payrolls and were filled with scorn for less savvy executives who were deemed to have "overpaid" for baseball talent. In a way, all of this was still rooting for laundry. It's just that the laundry consisted of a general manager's polo shirt instead of ballplayers' uniforms.

Another example of a more disconnected fandom can be seen via the phenomenon, most prevalent in hockey but present to lesser degrees elsewhere, in which fans and the media display a seeming insecurity about the status of the sport and make great efforts to promote it as somehow superior to other sports. This is most commonly seen in the form of boasts about how hockey players are tougher than other athletes. That they are not as easily sidelined by injuries as players in other sports and are less pampered, more blue-collar, and thus possess some greater moral worth than athletes in other sports. The subset of hockey fans and hockey media who traffic in this stuff seem unable to merely praise their sport. Rather, they find it necessary for their sport to be acknowledged as the *best* sport. In this, a fandom of something other than a team or a player is prioritized.

There is likewise an increasingly prevalent subset of college sports fandom that has sought to expand loyalty beyond that of a team and its players to the entire conference in which the team plays. Some Georgia fans root for Alabama in games the latter plays against Big Ten opponents because an Alabama victory in that game would shine reflected glory on the Southeastern Conference, thereby elevating Georgia's standing as well. Some Oklahoma fans root for Kansas to make a deep run in the NCAA tournament for the greater glory of the Big 12. Such rooting, often for one's bitter rivals, at the very least scrambles the idea of in-group and out-group identity that sports psychologists often cite as motivators for fans.

Perhaps the most disconnected brand of loyalty I've seen is associated with the NFL. For at least the past decade, commissioner Roger Goodell has made no secret of the fact that matters of business, television, marketing, public relations, league administration, and player discipline should all be viewed through the prism of "protecting the shield," referring to the trademarked shield-shaped logo of the league itself. "Protecting the shield" is Goodell's term describing his duty to the league, its image, and even its revenue. As a job security strategy, this makes some level of sense for Goodell personally, as it's literally his job to advance the interests of the league. However, the concept of "protecting the shield" has to some degree bled outside of the NFL's corporate offices, with Goodell's brand of deflection of criticism of the league becoming at least a secondarily defining feature for a number of fans as well. Indeed, the NFL now sells shield logo caps, T-shirts, and hoodies. Some people even buy them.

All of this—rooting for laundry, rooting for a front office and its executives, rooting for a sport as an abstract, superior pursuit, rooting for a conference, and rooting for the literal trademarked logo of the NFL—represents a mode of sports consumption that is a step or three removed from the appreciation and enjoyment of athletic performance or the participation in an in-group of like-minded fans. And that can lead to some strange reactions when things that happen on (or off) the field don't align with our personal ideals.

If you're like me (and most sports fans), you got into sports at a pretty young age. Maybe your mom or your dad or an older sibling liked sports, and you watched with them. Maybe you liked sports because they were entertaining and occasionally amazing and because it gave you things to talk about with your family and your friends. Or maybe you just realized early on that sports were, above all else, fun.

Because you were young when you got into sports, your appreciation of sports likely developed in something of a vacuum in which the real world did not intrude because, frankly, you didn't know all that much about the real world. Later, however, as your understanding of the world developed and your moral and ethical compass came online, you started to see all the ways in which the real world—often the ugliest parts of the real world—affected sports, sports teams, and the athletes who participate in them. Assuming you're not a master of compartmentalization and rationalization, when you started thinking about those real world issues in sports, you found yourself faced with what seems like a never-ending series of dilemmas:

- If you're a New York Yankees fan, and the Yankees are facing elimination in Game Seven of a playoff series, how might you feel if the starting pitcher for that game is Domingo Germán, who was suspended for eighty-one games in 2020 after he was found to have slapped his girlfriend at a charity gala, forcing her to lock herself in a closet and call for help? What about if the pitcher who comes on in relief after him is Aroldis Chapman, who in 2015 was accused of pushing his girlfriend, choking her, and then firing eight gunshots into a wall in anger?

- If you're an Oakland Athletics fan, does the fact that your team's last World Series title, in 1989, was undoubtedly powered by multiple players who were on steroids sit well with you?

- If you're a Brooklyn Nets fan, how do you reconcile your love for your team and its biggest star, Kevin Durant, with his usage of vile homophobic and misogynistic slurs while engaged in an internet beef in 2021? For that matter, how do you reconcile your basketball fandom with the fact that the NBA barely slapped Durant on the wrist for it?

- If you're an Atlanta Braves fan, what do you do with the fact that, for over thirty years, whenever your team is trying to rally late in a game, drumbeats and old-school, Hollywood-style "on the warpath" music blares from the PA system while fans whoop and make chopping motions with foam tomahawks? For that matter, what do you do with the fact that your team's nickname and iconography are based on racist Native American stereotypes that are over a century old?

- If you're a US tennis or soccer fan, does it bother you that the women in those sports—Serena Williams, Megan Rapinoe, Alex Morgan—are, without question, the best at what anyone in those sports have ever done, yet make far less money than their inferior male counterparts?

- If you're a baseball fan of any team, does it bother you that there are fewer Black players in the game now than there have been at almost any point since the game was fully integrated? Or that, despite the success of Black players and the significant number of Latino players in the game, the ranks of managers, coaches, and executives in the sport are overwhelmingly white?

- How does it feel when the owner of the team you root for donates large amounts of money to odious political candidates who espouse conspiracy theories, racism, and anti-Semitism?

- If you're a fan of the Houston Astros, do you wear your "2017 World Series Champions" T-shirt despite the fact that it has since been conclusively proven that the team cheated via an elaborate sign-stealing scandal to gain an edge on its opponents?

- What goes through your head when, while working on your March Madness bracket, you click on an article that reminds you that the NCAA typically pulls in about a billion dollars each year in revenue from media rights fees, ticket sales, corporate sponsorships, and TV ads, while all but a select few of the young men who do all the playing don't make a dime? How about that many of them could be run out of the game, and possibly out of their career, because they accepted a free meal from the wrong person?

- If you're a football fan of any team and at any level, how do you watch players repeatedly slam into one another, often head-to-head, knowing what we now know about chronic traumatic encephalopathy (CTE) and other brain trauma that have been linked with depression, dementia, and suicide?

It's not like any of these things are unique or isolated incidents. At one point or another, any team can be impacted by these sorts of things. Hundreds of players have been credibly accused of domestic violence, racism, homophobia, or misogyny, with some of them pulling off exactas or even trifectas across those categories. Scandals of all stripes have affected all sports, all leagues, and all teams. Inequality between men's and women's sports is pervasive. The damage done to the minds and bodies of players for our entertainment sometimes makes them more akin to gladiators than athletes. The billionaire class that owns and runs professional sports is full of odious characters with odious ethics.

There isn't a lot you can do with some of these things. You can and certainly should stop supporting abusers and racists, and you can and certainly should do what is possible to use their bad acts as a basis for learning, teaching, and advocacy. Some of these sorts of things can, quite reasonably, make you question whether you want to continue to be a fan of a team or, possibly, even an entire sport altogether.

In the end, though, problems like racism, sexism, cheating, the strong exploiting the weak, and people possessing generally bad politics are way bigger than sports and are certainly not unique to them. We're certainly not going to be able to solve them just in the context of sports.

But we can fight back against some of the dilemmas raised above. When the sports-industrial complex uses your loyalty for its own ends, it is our responsibility as fans to call them out. In the next few chapters, we'll explore the most egregious examples of this fan exploitation in more depth.

2
WINNING ISN'T EVERYTHING

In 2019, *USA Today* published a story about the fiftieth anniversary of the World Series champion 1969 Mets. The story featured interviews with '69 Mets stars Cleon Jones, Bud Harrelson, Art Shamsky, and others about the "Amazin'" title run of what had been, to that point, baseball's worst team.

The nostalgic remembrances from the men who won the title were enjoyable, but as often happens with stories like these, the writer took things too far and oversold his case. He referred to the Mets not just as a winners who helped a generation of New York baseball fans forge wonderful sports memories but as saviors of an entire city as well:

> They will gather together in New York later in June, rehashing stories from 50 years ago, reminiscing about the year they turned the baseball world upside down, becoming perhaps the most beloved team in history.

The 1969 Mets.

The team that helped revitalize a city in ruins and heal a nation in turmoil, showing the world you can turn the inconceivable to the improbable to the possible to the incredible, in a way only sports can possibly do.

Now would be a good time to remember that the city the Mets allegedly "revitalized" found itself on the brink of bankruptcy well into the 1970s and experienced poverty, urban decay, and spiking crime rates for the next twenty-five years. It would also be a good time to remember that, in just the year after the final out of the 1969 World Series, the nation the Mets allegedly "healed" witnessed Altamont, the escalation of bombing of Cambodia, the Kent State shootings, the Weather Underground bombings, the police killing of reporter Ruben Salazar at a Chicano anti-war demonstration, New York's Hard Hat Riot, and a bunch of other extraordinarily crappy things. Over fifty years later, one still has a hard time finding anything, specifically, the New York Mets healed, and that includes the New York Mets franchise itself, which has mostly been a tire fire since then.

Yes, I am being flippant, but I do so to illustrate how eye-rollingly superficial "[sports team] healed [city/nation]" narratives invariably are. Such stories are, generally, a broad-brush paint job in which the source of strife—poverty, crime, economic challenges, natural disaster, terrorism, etc.—is paired with the local sports team's subsequent title run, which is cast as a spiritual balm. The words "heal" and "uplift" are pretty common in these stories.

Most of these stories follow the same pattern:

- A montage of the strife in whatever its form (bonus if it's from the 1960s and you can reuse some existing "turbulent '60s" B-roll and run Buffalo Springfield's "For What It's Worth" behind it);

- A chronicling of the sports team's run; and

- A declaration that everything was better after that.

We see these sorts of things whenever a team from a down-on-its-luck place has a title run or serves as host to a major sporting event. The Detroit Tigers, Red Wings, and Pistons have all gotten this treatment, with their championships alleged to have alleviated urban unrest, widespread poverty, and disinvestment. The Boston Red

Sox are almost always centered when discussing the 2013 Boston Marathon bombing. There is no shortage of other instances in which the fortunes of a city are conflated with the fortunes of a city's sports teams.

A classic example of this involves a common telling of the story of the World Series champion 1968 Detroit Tigers and the alleged "healing" role they played for the city a year after the 1967 Detroit riot that left forty-six dead, nearly 2,000 injured, and over 2,500 businesses burned to the ground. When discussed in connection with that Tigers team, the riot tends to merely provide the backdrop for a story about a championship baseball team that brought a divided city together. A story of Americans at odds over race and class coming together over the national pastime. A story in which the city feared another large scale uprising in 1968 and, when that did not happen, the Tigers' 1968 World Series run *ipso facto* "helped heal the city."

The Tigers clinched the American League pennant with a 2–1 win over the New York Yankees on September 17, 1968. The next morning, the *Detroit Free Press* reported in a front page story, "For one brief, shining moment after Detroit won the American League pennant, blacks and whites mingled in color-blind joy, thousands strong, on the streets of downtown Detroit." Later that week, Detroit sports columnist Joe Falls wrote to a national audience in the *Sporting News*, "My city needed a release; it needed an outlet to release its pent-up emotions. It found it in a baseball team, men playing a boy's game." As recounted by Patrick Harrigan in his 1997 book, *The Detroit Tigers: Club and Community 1945–1995*, three weeks later, after the Tigers defeated the St. Louis Cardinals in the World Series, team owner John Fetzer told team manager Mayo Smith, "You've not only won the pennant and the series, you might have saved the city." Those words were echoed later in the 2002 HBO Sports documentary *A City on Fire: The Story of the '68 Detroit Tigers,* the conclusory words of which were that the team "may not have saved the Motor City, but there's little doubt they helped it to heal."

This telling, however, was not given serious credence by people who actually paid attention to the real situation within Detroit at the time or who understand what has happened in Detroit since. A prominent Detroit psychiatrist named Paul Lowinger was asked at the time about the joy and notable lack of violence apparent in the city in the days after the Tigers clinched the pennant and subsequently won the World Series. Lowinger told the *Detroit Free Press* that the apparent harmony in the city was a "happy release of a sense of anger," but that it was a merely temporary one, saying, "It's a good feeling while it lasts; it's just like church. The thing is, they don't take it home. I refuse to be optimistic about it. If it takes a pennant and World Series to do it, God help us, we're that bad off. A pennant happens only once in twenty-three years." Despite that, the "Tigers healed Detroit" narrative is often deployed by Tigers fans to this day, even by those who in other contexts fully acknowledge what actually happened in Detroit afterward. It's almost as if Mickey Lolich winning three games against the Cardinals didn't do anything to actually heal racial resentment and distrust or stem the white flight and massive disinvestment in the city that cost it people, cost it jobs, and cost it tax revenues while poverty, crime, and despair reigned for the next several decades.

Another notable example of a sports team being cited as a healing force is the NFL's New Orleans Saints in the wake of Hurricane Katrina. In August 2005, the Saints' home, the Louisiana Superdome, gained international attention when it housed thousands of people seeking shelter, becoming the focal point of the humanitarian crisis and the US government's failure to properly and responsibly respond to the disaster. The building suffered extensive damage as a result of the storm and as a result of the human misery which took place inside. The Saints were forced to play their entire season on the road, splitting "home" games between San Antonio's Alamodome, Louisiana State University's Tiger Stadium in Baton Rouge, and one game at Giants Stadium in East Rutherford, New Jersey.

The Saints returned to playing all of their regular home games of the 2006 season at a repaired and refurbished Superdome. Early in their first game back in New Orleans, Saints player Steve Gleason blocked a punt, which teammate Curtis Deloatch recovered in the Atlanta Falcons' end zone for a touchdown. The Saints won the game and, after a horrible 3–13 season the year before, went on to have the most successful campaign in franchise history up to that time, reaching the NFC Championship Game. Three years later, the Saints defeated the Indianapolis Colts to win Super Bowl XLIV, the franchise's first-ever championship. In July 2012, a statue depicting Gleason blocking the punt entitled "Rebirth" was erected outside the Superdome. A news report at the time commented that the blocked punt "etched Steve Gleason into Saints lore and became symbolic of New Orleans' resilience in the face of disaster."

Over time, the Saints have gone from being cited as a mere "symbol" of resilience to an actual, substantive factor in the city's comeback, at least by certain people. A story on CNBC in 2015, for example, noted how the Saints "helped lift the city's spirits, and even boosted its fortunes in the long run." The story seems to mean the city's literal fortunes, citing the rebound in business at a couple of restaurants and bars near the stadium as evidence. It likewise quoted someone who claimed that "[t]heir influence on the city is infectious." The evidence of that influence infecting others? That same person "giving back to the Saints when he bought season tickets for the return year to the Superdome." It's worth noting, however, that the Saints were not in any way willing, at least initially, to serve as a "symbol of resilience." Indeed, the team's owner, Tom Benson, spent several months in the wake of Katrina working behind the scenes in an effort to move the Saints to another city entirely.

The Saints had set up temporary headquarters and a practice facility in San Antonio, and Benson was reportedly working with San Antonio's mayor and Texas governor Rick Perry to make that city its new permanent home. There were likewise rumors that the NFL, while publicly declaring that it wanted the Saints to go back to New Orleans, privately preferred them to move to Los Angeles, which did not have a team at that time, or perhaps Toronto, in service of the league's long-standing interest in making inroads into the Canadian market. In early October, a report emerged that Benson fired a team vice president who would not agree to accept money from him in order to keep discussions about a possible permanent relocation confidential. Soon after that report, the Saints played an October 2005 game in Baton Rouge at which Benson was jeered by fans angry about the rumors. Benson left the game early, later claiming that he and his family were in danger due to the abuse.

Over the next few months, it became apparent that repairs to the Superdome would, contrary to initial expectations, be completed in time for the 2006 season. Benson, less able to justify a move based on the suitability of the stadium, and subject to increased public pressure, agreed to keep the team in New Orleans, paving the way for the Saints to serve as a "symbol of resilience." It was an extraordinarily limited symbol, to be sure, given that New Orleans's post-Katrina rebuild and recovery has been accompanied by profound racial and economic inequality, with whiter, more affluent neighborhoods seeing considerably more investment and rebuilding than Blacker and poorer neighborhoods did, and leading to a diaspora of nearly 100,000 of New Orleans's pre-Katrina Black population. But hey, the sports bars and Saints season ticket holders are doing pretty good.

There are really no practical limits to the sorts of civic tragedies certain people will claim professional sports can fix. The most appalling one I've yet seen happened where I live, in Columbus, Ohio, in late 2020.

On December 4, 2020, a Franklin County sheriff's deputy shot a Black man, Casey Goodson Jr., killing him with five shots to the back. There was no obvious reason why the deputy confronted Goodson to begin with. He was not armed. He was not a criminal suspect. The deputy, in fact, had been called to the neighborhood on a completely unrelated matter. Goodson was merely walking into his grandmother's home, carrying a sandwich, when the deputy shot and killed him. As is so often the case in police killings of Black people, the deputy was not wearing a body camera, and the official reports in the immediate aftermath of the killing were contradictory and lacked transparency.

A little over a week after Goodson's killing, Columbus's Major League Soccer team, the Columbus Crew, defeated the Seattle Sounders to win the MLS Championship game. The following morning, the CEO of the Columbus

Foundation—a charitable fund founded by and run by the wealthy and powerful elite of the city—sent the following in a letter to its members:

> A week of blood, sweat, and tears. Blood spilled in the fatal shooting in the back of Casey Goodson, Jr., a tragic loss for his family and for our community. Sweat on the brows of the medical community, trying their almighty best to save us, in some cases from ourselves, while Ohio surged 41% in coronavirus cases this week alone. Tears in the form of those trying to juggle so much, to hold on to their homes, to find food, and educate their children.
>
> And then, today, we wake up to the fact that we have become once again a Championship City as the Columbus Crew, a team of diverse, international—and local—talent willed their way to overcome the odds against them to win the MLS Cup.
>
> We needed that good news, and in that case the sweat and tears of victory at the end of another week of tragedy, hardship, loss, and dread. The Crew's display of grit and determination and

skill, and the community support that made their existence even possible today, is indeed inspiring. And, I am thankful to all involved, as they remind us of what we are capable of as we put our minds to it.

So, as the effort, goals, smoke and songs of a championship victory go from exhilarating experience to cherished memory, let us resolve to be everyday champions of justice, of passion, of kindness, and generosity so that we can write the history of our community in this time as one for all.

In the CEO's defense, he didn't *directly* claim that the Crew winning the MLS title made the killing of Casey Goodson Jr. and the grief it caused *better*. But he certainly did claim that the soccer team winning made the people who get letters from the CEO of the Columbus Foundation *feel* better. It cast an unjustified police killing and a soccer championship together as if they were just the normal yin and yang of the week, with the soccer team putting all of that unpleasantness to rest, thank God. It's also worth noting that the line in the letter about how "community support" made the Columbus Crew's "existence even possible today" was, to those familiar with the team's recent history, a gratuitous defense of the Columbus Foundation's role in rallying support for taxpayer dollars to be used in the construction of a new stadium for the team, which had previously been on the brink of moving to Austin, Texas. If one were the sort who is not inclined to be all that charitable when it comes to the words and deeds of the business leaders and their wealth-driven philanthropy, one might construe this communication as saying, "See? If we hadn't gotten our way with the publicly funded stadium, this city would still be sad about that murder. And now, thanks in part to us, it's not."

In this case, at least the "sports-make-everything-better" narrative did not last for years like it has in New Orleans or Detroit. Indeed, the letter led to a pretty big outcry once it traveled beyond the Columbus Foundation's distribution list. Less than twenty-four hours after it was sent, the CEO apologized, tweeting that "[t]he taking of his life was singularly tragic and to put his death in a shared context of any other community challenges and events was an error. I meant to honor Casey and his family, but I understand I failed to do so."

Whatever the details, most of these sports-heal-civic-wounds narratives have the same sorts of flaws. At best, they overstate the significance of sports in society, presuming that happiness among ticket-buying sports fans—who are usually whiter and better off than your average city resident who may be the one in need of "healing"—means broad-based happiness among the populace. More commonly, they simply ignore the actual city or society beyond anything but its most superficial markers. It's not even a matter of correlation and causation being confused. There's very rarely any evidence presented that the sports made the underlying problems any better to begin with. All one usually gets from these things is a sense that, at least to the sports commentator/documentarian telling the story and to the people who closely followed the sports team, things were good.

This is not to say that sports mean *nothing* in this context. Sports success can certainly make a lot of people happy, even people hit hard by adversity, at least temporarily. People only tangentially connected to the strife in question may also decide that a sporting event "healed" a city. For example, if something bad happened in your city but didn't affect you directly, you may believe that the trophy-hoisting put a nice bookend on the trauma that was more directly felt by others. And, of course, individuals directly connected with the sporting events in question, like Cleon Jones, who was quoted in the Mets example, can experience a more lasting change in their lives as a result of this sort of success that they might see as general uplift.

That's not the same thing as healing, though. Because while you or I can close that chapter on it all when the game is over, survivors of traumatic events and victims of systematic oppression or chronic strife cannot and do not do so that easily. There were people still hurting in Detroit after 1968, in New York (and the nation) after 1969, in New Orleans after the Saints won the Super Bowl, and in Columbus after the Crew won their title. The very best that can be said of a given sports triumph amid civic adversity is that it was a pleasant, albeit temporary distraction. But not everyone had the luxury of enjoying that temporary distraction. And a distraction is not the same thing as a cure.

Columbus in 2020 won't be the last time you see this pattern play out. It will repeat itself over and over until the end of organized sports. It will repeat itself as long as there are people who conflate the fortunes of a city with the fortunes of a city's sports teams. And because the sports-industrial complex relies so heavily on leveraging misguided notions of civic loyalty and allegiance, there will always—always—be people who do that.

3
THE STADIUM SCAM

There's a line from the 1989 movie *Field of Dreams* that almost everybody knows, even if they haven't seen the movie. Except most people don't *actually* know it. Almost everyone gets it wrong.

The line is *not*, "If you build it, *they* will come." It is, "If you build it, *he* will come." The ghost or whatever it is that's living in Ray Kinsella's cornfield, imploring him to build a baseball diamond, is not promising *many* people. It's promising one person, Ray's dad. And though Ray and his friend Terence Mann later talk about charging people by the carload to visit the new ballpark and save Ray's struggling farm, the ghost's motive is not financial.

Sports fans similarly get the motives of the sports-industrial complex wrong whenever it says it wants to get a new ballpark or stadium built, usually with taxpayer dollars. Except in those instances, it's because the sports-industrial complex is not merely misunderstood like the ghost out in the corn. It's usually lying. It's leveraging fans' civic pride by promising copious financial benefits for the city. It's also leveraging fans' allegiance to the team by promising on-the-field glory if only they can see fit to pony up a billion bucks or more for the new facility.

There are scores of examples of ballpark, stadium, and arena projects built on empty promises of boosting the local economy, complete with dubious "economic impact" studies that purport to show how crowds on game days will bring new spending on restaurants, hotels, and shops, raising the city's profile. Those studies, though, are woefully, even comically flawed, aimed as they are to sway public officials and the opinion of voters who need to approve such projects—assuming the public is even in the loop—rather than to reflect economic reality. Sound economic research, in contrast, finds that taxpayer subsidized sports stadiums usually result in a *net negative* overall economic impact. Despite that, cities, counties, and states have funded stadium projects so regularly that we've begun thinking of them as public facilities like roads or schools, likely because the teams that call those stadiums home share the city or state name and, when it suits them at least, portray themselves as almost quasi-civic institutions.

To be sure, hosting a professional sports franchise does have some legitimate public benefits, even if they're intangible. Strangers come together to cheer on victories and commiserate over losses. Sports give people with disparate backgrounds, lifestyles, and ideologies something in common which, theoretically at least, smooths over the differences among us. Professional sports franchises can serve as a local amenity that can improve a city's quality of life, at least in some ways. When Oklahoma City voters approved millions of dollars in public spending for renovating the city's arena in order to lure the NBA franchise that became the Oklahoma City Thunder, civic leaders cast that aspect of it—making Oklahoma City a "big league city" and "putting it on the map"—as the primary goal. While it's hard to measure what being "a big league city" actually does for a city, it's certainly the case that people generally think differently about a city with a major league professional team in it than one without one. Oklahoma City was at least being honest about its intentions.

Usually, though, "putting the city on the map" is not the aim of these new or renovated stadiums, and it's not the focus of the pitch. Usually, the promise is that the new facility will be an economic boon to the community and that it will help keep the team competitive. In some cases, it's less a promise than a threat: if you *don't* pay for this new stadium, the team will skip town entirely. No matter what the pitch is, when it comes time to fund the new stadium, they're *your* Mudville Nine. When the revenues created by that new stadium begin pouring in, however, they're Mudville Nine LLC. Those revenues are almost always retained by the owners of the team, and the taxpayers are almost always left holding the bag.

It wasn't always like this, though. There were a small handful of publicly funded sports facilities before the 1950s, but these were mostly intended for a grander civic use than just being the home for professional sports teams. They were built for the Olympics, or national or worldwide exhibitions. They often had an open-ended horseshoe shape, which might enable grand parades or allow the stadium to be utilized for any number of public purposes. In contrast, if a pro team's owner wanted a new ballpark, stadium, or arena just to have a new one, he simply built it, the same way a factory owner builds a factory, or a shipping company builds a warehouse.

That changed when authorities in Milwaukee County, Wisconsin, built County Stadium in the early 1950s.

While ostensibly built for the minor league Milwaukee Brewers, who had called the city home for decades, the county hoped to use the new facility to attract a Major League Baseball franchise. They were successful in doing so, too, getting the Braves to leave Boston and move into County Stadium prior to the 1953 season. The minor league version of the Brewers, in fact, would never get a chance to play at the new stadium.

The Braves' move to Milwaukee was the first of several relocations in baseball over the next decade. The St. Louis Browns moved to Baltimore to become the Orioles in 1954. The Brooklyn Dodgers and New York Giants moved to Los Angeles and San Francisco, respectively, in 1958. The Washington Senators moved to Minnesota to become the Twins in 1961. These moves were not instances in which a new publicly funded stadium, in and of itself, enticed a team to relocate, but they all revolved around the idea of exploiting new markets and searching for new revenues, and they all caused public officials to appreciate that what had been a static professional sports landscape in which teams stayed in one city and one stadium for decades on end was not an immutable state of affairs. Teams could move if they wanted to, and a big justification for teams to move was because their facilities were no longer up to snuff.

In the 1960s and early 1970s, partially inspired by the demands of professional sports teams for new ballparks and stadiums and partially inspired by a spirit of urban renewal, many cities planned and built multipurpose stadiums to replace their old baseball-only and football-only predecessors. These facilities, like most public works, had bang-for-their-buck in mind. One piece of land and one building to support both the local baseball and the local football team saved money, and, at least in theory, what would have been spent to support the infrastructure for two stadiums could be spent elsewhere. These new places, located as they were next to freeways and surrounded by seas of parking lots, also catered to a country that was increasingly built around cars. They may have been publicly funded homes for privately owned sports teams, but they were decidedly austere buildings that had utility, not luxury, principally in mind. These new facilities, often called "cookie-cutter stadiums," served their purpose, but they were never loved. Indeed, team owners began referring to them as "antiquated" as early as the 1970s, and calls for their replacement began as early as the 1980s.

Then, in 1984, something pretty shocking happened in Baltimore that changed everything.

By the early 1980s, the NFL's Baltimore Colts had been agitating for a new stadium for some time. Memorial Stadium, which they shared with the Orioles, was originally one of those horseshoe-shaped, public-parade-ground-type places but had been rebuilt into a very early version of a multiuse facility when the Orioles moved from St. Louis in 1954. As a stadium, the rebuilt Memorial Stadium was neither fish nor fowl, lacking both the beauty and grandeur of classic ballparks and the scale of interwar-era parade ground stadiums but also lacking the utility of the cookie-cutters. Heeding the calls of two different Colts owners—the team changed hands from Carroll Rosenbloom to Robert Irsay in 1972—Baltimore mayor William Schaefer and Maryland governor Marvin Mandel created a stadium committee that came up with a proposal to build a modern domed stadium for the two teams, nicknamed the "Baltodome." The proposal, however, didn't go anywhere. And it didn't merely fail to gain any support to pass the Maryland legislature. Indeed, Baltimore's city comptroller actually had an amendment to the city's charter placed on the ballot in 1974 that would prohibit the use of public funds to replace Memorial Stadium at all. The measure passed 56 to 44 percent. The message was clear: Baltimore would not, under any circumstances, use taxpayer funds to give the Colts and Orioles a new stadium.

Defeated in his effort to get a new stadium, for the next several years, Colts owner Robert Irsay met with out-of-state mayors and governors, many of whom were eager to give him what Baltimore and Maryland would not. And he was not secretive about it.

"I like Baltimore and want to stay there, but when are we going to find out something about our stadium?" Irsay said in 1977. "I'm getting offers from towns like Indianapolis to build me a new stadium and give me other inducements to move there. I don't want to, but I'd like to see some action in Baltimore." Irsay would play the cities making him offers off one another too, shuttling between Phoenix and Indianapolis, telling each city that he would be happy to move the Colts there and getting sweeter and sweeter offers every time he came to town. The overtures actually inspired Indianapolis to begin building a domed stadium—the Hoosier Dome—before there was even a team committed to play in it. It was like Milwaukee in the 1950s all over again, but this time it was a team making demands on cities as opposed to cities taking it upon themselves to attract a team.

On March 29, 1984, with the Hoosier Dome all but ready for, well, anyone, the Maryland legislature suddenly became concerned that the Colts might actually bolt, and they began the process of taking possession of the team by eminent domain. In response, Irsay had all of the Colts' equipment and office supplies loaded onto moving trucks and driven to Indianapolis in the dark of night. The Colts remain there to this day and, despite Cleveland Browns owner Art Modell moving his team to Baltimore to become the Ravens twelve years later, there are many in Baltimore who are still devastated by the loss of their team.

The Colts' move to Indianapolis had far greater significance than upsetting Baltimore football fans, however. It set a precedent in which a professional sports team could threaten a city with abandonment if they didn't get a new taxpayer-funded stadium, play would-be new homes against one another for the sweetest possible offers, and, if the home city didn't pony up, simply leave town. The key to this play—the only thing that makes it work—is the exploitation of fan loyalty and the transforming of fans into lobbyists in service of the stadium push. The motivation is a function of the sports-industrial complex convincing fans that there could be nothing worse on Earth than their local team leaving town and using that sentiment to bully local officials into writing massive checks.

All of this is despite the fact that, most of the time, the actual threat to move is implausible. Realistically speaking, there are a finite number of viable alternative markets for most teams. Ask yourself: were the Yankees really going to leave New York when they shook the city down to build their latest version of Yankee Stadium? The emotional and sometimes political fallout of the very few contested relocations that have happened, such as Robert Irsay moving the Colts and, three decades prior, Walter O'Malley moving the Dodgers from Brooklyn to LA, has been so great that reason rarely enters into these conversations. Fans don't want to lose their teams. Local officials don't want to be the ones who let the team leave town. The gun put to their head by the sports-industrial complex often has no bullets, but placing it there usually works.

The number of teams who have employed this gambit or who, at the very least, nodded at another team doing it and got a new playground from locals without even needing to make the threat, outnumbers those who either stayed in their old, venerable ballparks or, even more rarely, paid the freight for their new digs themselves. Between 1970 and 2019, public funding for professional sports facilities in the United States totaled $32.5 billion, covering approximately 65 percent of total stadium costs. When you add in necessary infrastructure such as new freeway off-ramps, upgraded utilities, and the like, it's likely a few billion more. The vast majority of those dollars came after 1984, when Jim Irsay showed that an unsatisfied team might pack up and take off.

Some of those deals have been better than others for taxpayers, but none of them have been particularly good. And the worst of them have been downright appalling. What follows is a mere sampling.

Minnesota Vikings

The Minnesota Vikings' new stadium, US Bank Stadium, was the product of Vikings owner Zygi Wilf threatening Governor Mark Dayton that he'd move the team if the state didn't pay for it. The threats first involved using a couple of suburbs as leverage, unveiling stadium plans that were likely never going to happen but that nonetheless pressured Minneapolis officials. Then, Wilf brought in NFL commissioner Roger Goodell to make noises about how great it'd be if a team—any team, but maybe the Vikings!—would move to Los Angeles, which then did not have an NFL franchise. In the end, Minnesota blinked and coughed up $678 million of the $1.1 billion construction costs.

Maybe the "best" part of the Vikings stadium deal, though, has to do with birds.

US Bank Stadium is a dramatic-looking place, encased in glass. When its design was revealed years before construction even began, conservation groups were concerned that the glass would cause birds to fly into it, killing themselves. Conservationists requested a bird-friendly design that used slightly less transparent bird-safe glass to avoid the problem, but such glass would've added about $1 million to construction costs. The Vikings and the state rejected the idea. Since the place opened, there have, in fact, been a large number of bird deaths, with some estimates holding that the stadium has killed more than twice as many birds as any other building in Minnesota during that time. As such, the state conducted a study—which would not have been necessary if they had listened to conservationists to begin with—and now the cost of retrofitting the stadium with bird-safe glass stands at $10 million. It is unclear if or when that fix will be made, but it's added money on the taxpayers' tab.

Arizona Coyotes

When the old version of the NHL's Winnipeg Jets moved to Arizona to become the Phoenix Coyotes, the team played in a downtown arena that they shared with the NBA's Phoenix Suns. While lots of hockey and basketball teams share homes, the Coyotes didn't have to for long because the suburb of Glendale was on a years-long sports facility-building bender, and the Coyotes benefited from it.

Between the mid-1990s and mid-2000s, Glendale footed 75 percent of the bill on a half-billion-dollar football stadium for the Arizona Cardinals and paid millions more for a spring training facility for MLB's Chicago White Sox and Los Angeles Dodgers. In 2003, Glendale built what is now named Gila River Arena. Not only did the city pay for the place, but for years, it actually paid the Coyotes to manage the arena for them. Would that we all got such deals from our landlords.

The problem: most of the Coyotes' fans live in the East Valley of Phoenix, while Glendale sits in the West Valley. Given the sprawl of the Phoenix area, that meant most fans had to drive well over an hour through gnarly rush-hour traffic to get to a 7:00 p.m. faceoff. Attendance was predictably anemic, and the Coyotes suffered financially. Indeed, they regularly did not make even their fairly cheap rent payments to Glendale on time. (They did, of course, continue to collect their management fee like clockwork.) It's probably also worth mentioning that Glendale has routinely lost money on the Cardinals' football stadium deal too, making less from football than its debt service on the building and losing extra money every few years when the NFL schedules the Super Bowl for Glendale, requiring the city to make extra expenditures for the special event.

Around 2015, the Coyotes, fed up with losing money, began making noises about wanting a new arena or perhaps even a new city. To that end, they rejected Glendale's desire to enter into a new fifteen-year lease and instead signed only a one-year lease, all while taking meetings with officials from Las Vegas and suburban mayors from the East Valley of Phoenix. To their credit, Glendale officials called their bluff, happily entering into six straight one-year leases rather than bending over backward to give the hockey team what it wanted. In August 2021, Glendale, tired of dealing with the Coyotes, finally terminated its lease with the team, effective at the end of the 2021–22 season.

Cincinnati Reds and Bengals

Major League Baseball's Reds and the NFL's Bengals had shared the cookie-cutter Riverfront Stadium from its opening in 1970. By the mid 1990s, however, with multipurpose stadiums falling out of favor, each team wanted its own place. For their part, the Bengals threatened that if they did not get a new stadium, they might move to Baltimore, which was at the time still smarting from the loss of the Colts but had not yet enticed the Cleveland Browns to come there and become the Ravens.

While the Bengals' threat seemed implausible for several reasons, and while the Reds never threatened to move at all, Hamilton County, Ohio, was nonetheless happy to oblige. County commissioners pitched the idea as a trade: if voters would agree to a sales tax increase to pay off construction bonds, the commission would roll back the property tax rates. Even on the surface, that's a pretty bad deal, as increased sales taxes disproportionately impact the poor and property tax cuts disproportionately benefit wealthy property owners, but the deal would get even worse over time.

The price of the two stadiums swelled, as they always do, because preconstruction estimates are almost always understated. The portion allocated to the football stadium, some $350 million, was at the time the largest-ever public subsidy for an NFL stadium. As a result of the escalating costs and far lower sales tax revenues than expected, the county has faced steep debt payments for years, with debt service eating up as much as 17 percent of the county's entire annual budget for just two buildings, one of which is only in use eight to ten times a year. As a result, the county slashed funding for public services like schools, the sheriff's department, and youth programs. It was even forced to sell a hospital it had owned for nearly a century. Eventually, the county repealed the property tax reduction that was the carrot to get residents to approve the stadiums in the first place, so no one got what they wanted—except the Bengals and the Reds.

Atlanta Braves

The Braves had called Turner Field home since 1997. That park, which was retrofitted from the stadium used for the 1996 Olympics, was still younger than half the parks in baseball when, in 2013, the Braves announced that the franchise would leave Turner Field for a new park in suburban Cobb County, Georgia. Their cited reasons for needing a new park related to capital improvements they claimed Turner Field needed but, really, was tied up in the fact that Cobb County allowed the possibility for the Braves to own and anchor a massive real estate development now known as the Battery, underwritten at the county's expense.

That new park, now known as Truist Park, ended up costing $1.4 billion, with Cobb County borrowing nearly $400 million in bonds paid for out of residents' property taxes. The deal was sealed in less than two weeks after word emerged that the Braves planned to move. How did such a massive project get put together so quickly? Easy: the county commission circumvented public records laws, preventing the public from having any input.

Braves president John Schuerholz spoke to the Atlanta Press Club after the deal was announced and admitted that approval for the $400 million subsidy would not have been possible if the public, you know, had known anything about it. Here's Schuerholz speaking in late 2013:

> "It didn't leak out. If it had leaked out, this deal would not have gotten done. . . . If it had gotten out, more people would have started taking the position of, 'We don't want that to happen. We want to see how viable this was going to be,' Schuerholz said. 'We were able to get that all done.'"

And get it done they did, though not without inconveniencing and alienating a hell of a lot of taxpayers and Braves fans in the process.

Cobb County taxpayers were hit by virtue of the simple nature of the deal. Because the project represented a diversion of funds from an existing tax instead of a new one, voters did not have a say on the matter. At the same time, other previously voter-approved expenditures for things like parks and libraries were cut because, sorry, the money needed to go the Braves and their new stadium. Braves fans who actually live in Atlanta, as opposed to Cobb County and the other northern Atlanta suburbs, meanwhile, have been geographically cut off due to the fact that the new park is separated from the city by a massively congested set of freeway interchanges and is inaccessible by public transportation. And make no mistake, this was by design.

At the time the Braves announced that they would be moving, the team released a map showing, in their view, where Braves fans lived precisely. The map was of the greater Atlanta area featuring red dots, each one indicating the home of Braves season ticket holders or people who purchased tickets online, which required that they give out their address. The bulk of those dots were concentrated in the suburban and exurban counties to the north of the city. The new stadium, the Braves claimed, would be better-positioned to serve its fans, who were, demographically speaking, older, whiter, richer, and more conservative than the city proper. Even if one were to ignore the fact that Braves fans who walked up to ticket windows or purchased tickets on the secondary market were not represented in that map, fans in the city of Atlanta—particularly Black fans—felt intentionally snubbed by the decision to move, with their views on the matter inevitably colored by decades of segregation and other forms of racial tension between the largely Black city and its largely white suburbs. This dynamic has led critics of the Braves to refer to Truist Park as "White Flight Field."

In early 2021, sports economist J. C. Bradbury released the result of a study of the economic impact of Truist Park and found that while it and the surrounding development led to an increase of sales tax receipts for the county, the magnitude of the increase has been small and not statistically significant. Bradbury found that approximately one-third of those sales tax revenues are derived from the crowding out of other local economic activity—i.e., money spent at a Braves game comes at the expense of money that would have been spent elsewhere in the county—and that in total, the added sales tax collections fall far short of what taxpayers are paying to service the debt on the public subsidies that funded the stadium in the first place.

The examples of stadium scams presented above are just a sampling. I could easily include a dozen more. All of these stadium deals are bad for cities, counties, states, their taxpayers, and the teams' fans. Studies, like the J. C. Bradbury study mentioned above, consistently show that the deals never pay for themselves with increased tax receipts and economic benefits like teams and public officials promise. The projects are also often sold as job-creation vehicles. At first, yes, there may be some construction jobs that arise from the building of the stadiums themselves, but those jobs last only a few years. After that, the only jobs that remain are for stadium workers such as ticket sellers, vendors, custodians, and maintenance workers, which are often seasonal, almost always low-paid, and are not great in number. The highly paid athletes who work in the stadiums spend half of their seasons on the road, with taxes on those earnings being paid elsewhere. The seasonal nature of professional sports, player trades, and free agency usually means that the players, and often the executives who work for teams, do not put down local roots. This leads to what economists call "leakage" of money that doesn't stay in the local economy.

If these are such bad deals, why do they keep happening?

The simplest explanation is fear. Because team owners can pick up and move to a new city like the Baltimore

Colts did in 1984, mayors, county commissioners, and governors feel like they must give owners anything they want for fear of the potential political disaster they imagine might occur if they were to lose a team on their watch. Or, as was the case in Atlanta, local officials essentially conspire with the teams themselves in order to get the money pushed through because, well, they just want to. They do that because sports facilities are big, very obvious projects that politicians can point to and say, "See, we got something big done!" They stand as accomplishments, such as they are, which are easier for voters to see than some complicated program or abstract policy enactment.

On the less public side of these things, politicians use these sorts of deals as a means of ingratiating themselves to and enmeshing themselves with the business and real estate development classes who benefit from such projects and who possess immense political power and make big political donations in most cities. It's a class to which most sports team owners belong, either directly or tangentially, so there's a natural synergy at play as well. Through all of this, there are perks that accrue to politicians who ingratiate themselves to team owners, such as getting to throw the first pitch at a ball game or the chance to entertain donors in a basketball arena's luxury box. It explains why government officials quite often serve as a critical component of the sports-industrial complex.

Mostly, though, both public officials and team owners know they can get away with it because of the way fan loyalty works. Professional sports teams enjoy a strong amount of public favor, and the sports-industrial complex exploits this in support for projects with little or no public utility. The only way for the stadium scam to stop is for local elected officials and fan bases to stand together and say that they are not going to play that game anymore. To take away teams' ability to say, "We're going to leave if you don't give us what we want" because, simply put, they will have no place to go. The only way that could ever work, though, is if a critical number of fans examine and question their loyalty to the teams they support and appreciate that it is not a loyalty that is reciprocated by the teams themselves.

4
GENTRIFYING THE BLEACHERS

In February 2016, the New York Yankees introduced a website called the Yankees Ticket Exchange, where ticket holders could resell their tickets on the secondary market. The team claimed that the move was made to "further combat fraud and counterfeiting of tickets," but that didn't fool anyone. It was made to try to get StubHub out of the Yankees' secondary market in favor of the team's own service and capture some additional revenue over and above that which they got from the original sale of the tickets. There was something a bit more going on there, however, than mere revenue maximization. There was something classist afoot.

This became obvious when, the day after the announcement of the Yankees Ticket Exchange, the team's chief operating officer, Lonn Trost, said that it was also aimed at keeping the prices for premium tickets sufficiently high so that the Yankees' wealthy season ticket holders would not be forced to mingle with the masses. Here's Trost, speaking to *Newsday* about the perils of StubHub selling tickets at below face value:

> The problem below market at a certain point is that if you buy a ticket in a very premium location and pay a substantial amount of money. It's not that we don't want that fan to sell it, but that fan is sitting there having paid a substantial amount of money for a ticket and [another] fan picks it up for a buck-and-a-half and sits there, and it's frustrating to the purchaser of the full amount. . . . And quite frankly, the fan may be someone who has never sat in a premium location. So that's a frustration to our existing fan base.

That's right: Trost was worried that wealthy Yankees fans would be "frustrated" by having to sit with common people. That like some stockholder, their investment would be diluted by virtue of the presence of people who found a way to see a game at a cheaper price. Over the next few days, rumors swirled that this was not just worry on Trost's part but rather a function of the swells in the luxury sections having *told* Trost that they really didn't like it when the *hoi polloi* got too close. They're not just paying for good sight lines, you know—they're paying to be separated from the common fans.

It's not just a social separation. Like all modern stadiums, Yankee Stadium, which opened in 2009, has a great many expensive seats, but it has a section of ultra-expensive seats which are *physically* separated from the rest of the stadium. Seats in this section, called the "Legends Suite" despite the fact that they are not self-contained luxury boxes but rather open-air seats in the main seating bowl of the stadium, can cost as much as $2,600 a game at face value and average more than $500 apiece. In between the Legends Suite and the rest of the ballpark is a concrete barrier that has often been described as a "moat." Fans who do not have tickets for the Legends Suite are not allowed in. This includes the period before games when, at most ballparks anyway, fans traditionally stand along the railing behind the dugouts during batting practice and seek autographs. At Yankee Stadium, this standing room is reserved for Legends Suite ticket holders only.

The exclusivity of the new Yankee Stadium is not limited to the Legends Suite. There is also a "Champions"

Level that, while not allowing you to get past the Legends moat, does allow you to bypass the metal detectors outside of the stadium and enter via a private reception area that looks a lot like an upscale hotel lobby. Beyond those sections, the new Yankee Stadium has seventy-eight luxury boxes of the "skybox" variety, compared to only nineteen in the old, original Yankee Stadium. There are also multiple lounges and restaurant areas beneath the seats, which are limited to premium ticket holders. They're so nice, in fact, that the premium ticket holders often spend the bulk of the game there, eating food—hot dogs and hamburgers, yes, but also a raw bar and a revolving selection of other upscale dining options from some of New York's finest restaurants—and drinking drinks that are included with their ticket prices while sitting in plush armchairs and watching the ball game on large-screen TVs. There are even exclusive areas *within* these exclusive areas, the most exclusive being the Harman Lounge, which is a separate lounge area reserved for those with *front-row* Legends Suite tickets.

Yankee Stadium, while on the extreme end of luxury, is not unique in modern professional sports facilities, almost all of which cater to the wealthy in countless ways. Most of these features boil down to exclusivity, both in terms of who can go where inside of stadiums and in terms of who can even get inside stadiums in the first place. This is particularly apparent in baseball, where tickets have become increasingly more expensive and harder to come by over the past twenty years, primarily because there are simply fewer seats now than there have been for nearly a century.

Beginning in 1992, with the opening of Oriole Park at Camden Yards in Baltimore, and lasting until the opening of the Rangers' Globe Life Field in Arlington, Texas, baseball experienced an unprecedented building boom. In that time, twenty-one new major league ballparks were constructed for existing teams, two new ballparks were constructed for expansion teams, and two existing facilities came into use for expansion teams. Two teams, the Atlanta Braves and Texas Rangers, built *two* new ballparks in that span. While these parks have been noted mostly for their aesthetics—better sight lines than the old, multipurpose stadiums they mostly replaced, retro design flourishes, and overall character and charm—an equally notable trait is their reduced seating capacity. A handful of these newer parks, such as Progressive Field in Cleveland and Chase Field in Arizona, and some parks which were built before the boom, like Kauffman Stadium in Kansas City, have further decreased capacity in the past several years. Even accounting for baseball's expansion from twenty-six to thirty teams over that period, there are now millions fewer available seats over the course of a 162-game baseball season than there were thirty years ago.

Over that same period, the price of tickets has gone up dramatically. The normal rules of economics suggest that a higher price would *reduce* demand, but that hasn't happened. Indeed, baseball's overall attendance has gone up significantly since the ballpark building boom began. While immediate attendance gains, in defiance of higher prices, were likely due to the novelty effect of gleaming new ballparks, which attracted fans who simply want to check out the new building, the gains have lasted for many years. The most likely reason is that baseball tickets have become Veblen goods: those goods, as described by economist Thorstein Veblen—the man who coined the term "conspicuous consumption"—as those for which demand increases as the price increases because of their exclusive nature and appeal as a status symbol.

A current Yankees season ticket holder, at least one familiar with economic theory, may take issue with that characterization. A Veblen good, after all, is typically defined as one where quality is beside the point, where the appeal is based on perception and exclusivity as opposed to inherent worth. They might point to the wider, more comfortable seats of the new ballpark and compare them favorably to the metal bench seating of old ballparks and say they're getting more for their added financial outlay. They might note the numerous HD video monitors scattered around the stadium, which allow fans to see things up close, and the vastly increased number of concession and merchandise stands and other ballpark amenities and argue that, no, this is about quality, not about status symbols.

That may be the case on the very high end of things, where there are nice comfy seats that are close to the action. The problem is that there are very few of those seats. The vast majority of seats at the newer ballparks, which are still considerably more expensive than all the seats at old ballparks are actually, much farther away from the field than they were at the old ballparks they replaced. The upper decks are now separated from the playing field by two and sometimes three levels of luxury suites, pushing them significantly higher into the sky than upper decks used to be. Likewise, as a result of the elimination of support pillars that blocked the view of some fans in the lower decks in old ballparks, the upper decks are pushed further *back* from the playing surface as well. Pushing the upper decks back has allowed ballparks to install a greater number of lower deck seats, which are often considered premium and exclusive and are priced as such but, actually, a great many of them are farther back from the playing field than they ever were at the older stadiums. Indeed, at least the last third of lower-deck seats are farther away from the field now than the *upper*-deck seats used to be at the old ballparks, rendering those video monitors less of a luxury and more of a necessity. Cushier seats, wider aisles, and a wider selection of concessions are nice, but at the end of the day, a baseball fan goes to the ballpark to see a ball game. Those fans who are interested primarily in that and who have no interest in or who cannot afford the close-in, expensive seats and luxuries they provide are out of luck in the modern baseball stadium.

At least baseball fans can afford *bad* seats. In the NBA, the notion of affordability is quickly disappearing. This is most notable in the case of the Golden State Warriors, who moved from Oakland to a new arena in San Francisco called Chase Center at the beginning of the 2019–2020 season. While the Warriors' considerable success in recent years made their games a hot ticket even before the move, the prices in the new arena caused significant sticker shock. One long-term season ticket holder, whose story was reported in the *San Francisco Chronicle* in 2018, had held seats five rows up from the court in the old arena since 1974. When he purchased them, the tickets cost a few dozen dollars per game. As recently as the 1990s, they were less than a hundred dollars a game. In the final years in Oakland, they had risen to $370 a game, which still represented a nice discount from what new buyers would pay due to a long-term ticket holder loyalty program offered by the Warriors.

As Chase Center was under construction, this particular season ticket holder, like all of the other season ticket holders, was invited to a meeting with the team's sales department to discuss purchasing seats in the new arena. The new deal: a mandatory, one-time $36,000 "membership fee" simply to be entitled to purchase a ticket, with each ticket costing $600 a game, amounting to nearly $25,000 for a forty-one-game season. For one seat. *And* his complimentary parking was eliminated. *And* he would have to make a thirty-year commitment. If he did not agree to those terms—indeed, if he did not agree to them that very day, the team told him—they would offer his seats to someone else. He declined, ending his forty-five-year tenure as a Warriors ticket holder.

The Warriors, like all sports teams, have learned that they can get away with pricing out those fans who aren't there for the luxuries and that they can make significantly more on people who are. They have learned that by jacking up the prices and limiting their number of seats, a larger percentage than ever of which will be occupied by season ticket holders, corporate clients, or fans that are wealthy enough to pay above-face prices to scalpers and brokers, they are shutting out a large portion of their fan base from the stadium experience. The portion of the fan base shut out is, of course, the common, working-class fan. In their place are the executives or customers of companies that buy Legends Suite tickets or Warriors courtside seats or their equivalents as perks. Celebrities or tech moguls who sit behind the bench, behind home plate, or in a suite above the fifty-yard line who want to see and be seen. Professionals who view owning season ticket packages as a status symbol or proof that they have made it to a certain place in life and society. People who splurge on seats that cost ten or twenty times more than what they cost even a few years ago because they want to treat themselves to something special or want to separate themselves from the masses in nosebleed sections or those who can't afford to get into the stadium at all.

All of this, of course, is a reflection of what is happening in society at large.

While a small number of very rich people have always been able to keep themselves separate and apart from the masses, over the past couple of decades, a larger number of people have come to use money, technology, and education to insulate themselves from the sort of everyday life all citizens once lived. Elite status, VIP sections, priority lines, "Cadillac" healthcare plans, private schools, and all manner of other luxuries available to the professional, technological, and entrepreneurial classes have created a situation in which a larger swath of the well-educated and at least moderately well-to-do have come to comprise a separate class from the rest of the country. Situations in which people come together in common spaces such as train stations, post offices, hospitals, libraries, public schools, museums, and retail spaces have decreased dramatically. There was once a time in America where the class divisions we had were denied and diminished out of either shame or idealism born of the notion that the United States is not a class-based society, but today that conceit has been disposed of almost entirely, with "success" being increasingly equated with one's ability to buy one's way out of the public sphere altogether. We have made it so that those with access to the gifts of the technological age can do their shopping, their banking, and their interactions with the government via electronic means without ever having to encounter the general public or, at the very least, the part of the general public unlike themselves. The increasing power of a small handful of technology companies is exacerbating this trend, turning even basic acts of life, such as buying groceries, into a class-based pursuit.

Sports have followed this trend. The professional, technological, and entrepreneurial classes have come to expect the utmost in luxury, service, and, above all else, exclusivity in every other aspect of their lives, and they now expect it from sports as well. They demand ballparks, stadiums, and arenas that accentuate exclusivity. They want VIP parking and VIP entrances. They want exclusive seating tiers and clubs where they can network, where they can be seen, and which common fans cannot access. The sports-industrial complex has eagerly met this desire for exclusivity and has delivered it to fans who can afford it. And not just those, like the Yankees and the Warriors, who are located in cities where massive wealth resides. At least two NHL teams, four NBA teams, five Major League Baseball clubs, and fifteen NFL teams require the purchase of personal seat licenses—the more traditional name for the Warriors' "membership fee"—before fans are even allowed to buy the season tickets. The most expensive version of this is offered by the Dallas Cowboys, who demand six figures *per seat,* not for the cost of buying a ticket, but for the privilege of being given a chance to buy tickets.

These innovations have been tremendous moneymakers for sports franchises, but they have come at the expense of the overall stadium experience. AT&T Stadium, where the Cowboys play, has often been criticized as having a "road atmosphere at home" due to so many fans treating it more like a social gathering than a sporting event. The San Francisco 49ers' luxury-packed stadium in Santa Clara, California, has made the team a mint, but it often sits partially full on Sundays. Those well-appointed indoor lounges at Yankee Stadium, meanwhile, have created a bit of an optics problem, as the Legends Suite seats are constantly visible during Yankees broadcasts yet often conspicuously empty, especially during playoff games when the weather is cooler and the wealthy fans choose to warm themselves inside. It's enough to make one feel as though the *acquiring* of exclusive seats is the endgame here as opposed to watching sporting events. As if being able to tell people you're a season ticket holder is more important than the game itself. Players have noticed all of this too, with many citing the lack of crowd noise and energy in the newer, luxury-filled stadiums compared to their more egalitarian predecessors. Mariano

Rivera, the New York Yankees' Hall of Fame closer, even talked about it in his memoir, noting that compared to the old Yankee Stadium, the new ballpark "doesn't hold noise or home-team fervor." He wrote that the old Yankee Stadium "was our 10th man—a loud and frenzied cauldron of pinstripe passion, with a lot of lifers in the stands. Maybe I'm wrong, but it's hard to see that the new place can ever quite duplicate that."

From 1902 through 1911, the Cincinnati Reds played in the wonderfully named ballpark, "the Palace of the Fans." The idea that a stadium could be built with common fans in mind today, however, seems like an impossibility. Live sports have been transformed from events that welcomed blue-collar and white-collar people on equal terms and cut across social, economic, and racial boundaries to yet another thing geared toward the professional classes, the wealthy, and, increasingly, the one percent. The result: fans in the stands are far from representative of fan bases at large and far less invested in the games than the common fan. It's hard to escape the conclusion that the sports-industrial complex likes them more than it likes you.

5
THE BUSINESS OF LOSING

Jean-Jacques Rousseau didn't have football or baseball in mind when he was writing about social contracts 350 years ago, but as fans, we all at least subconsciously assume that there are some inherent rights and obligations that apply to the world of sports, right?

The most basic idea along these lines is that in exchange for our fandom and our support, teams will do their best to put a successful product on the field, on the pitch, on the court, or on the ice. Even if teams stumble, and even if they are consistently outmatched year in and year out, the people who run them and play for them are at least trying to win and that in the end, winning is the yardstick by which success is ultimately measured. When the team wins, fans will enjoy things more, they will watch or attend games in greater numbers and purchase more team merchandise, all of which financially benefits the team. These benefits then confer an obligation on the team to do things like keep fan-favorite players around, make sure the game-going experience remains enjoyable, and do other things to keep the winning going. When the team loses, they will be punished by a weakening of support and a reduction in revenue, and will thereby be incentivized to get things back on track.

The fans' obligation in all of this is pretty simple: they have to show up and make sure that winning—or, at the very least, good faith efforts to win—is indeed supported. If a team is at least moderately successful but still doesn't sell tickets or attract eyeballs, the team's owner may find that it makes little sense to keep owning the team and may try to sell it. Or they may decide that the team could do better in a different city. We've seen that play out many times in history, of course. Despite winning numerous pennants and a World Series title in the 1940s and 1950s, the lack of fan support was a big contributing factor to the Dodgers leaving Brooklyn for Los Angeles in 1958. The Braves moved twice, with the club first leaving Boston and then Milwaukee despite putting some very good teams on the field in the years not long before each relocation. More recently, the Montreal Expos, which had some excellent seasons, left to become the Washington Nationals. Eventually, there is a decent chance that the Tampa Bay

Rays will leave St. Petersburg, Florida, despite a great deal of success over the past fifteen years, because the economics just aren't working. Multiple NBA and NHL teams have relocated in recent years when the pastures did not end up being as green as the league and the owners first envisioned, such as the Vancouver Grizzlies, the original iteration of the Charlotte Hornets, the Atlanta Thrashers, and the Quebec Nordiques. The NFL's Cardinals have moved twice, first from Chicago to St. Louis and then from St. Louis to Phoenix, both times because they really could not gain much support compared to more popular teams in their city.

Yes, in all of those situations there were complicating factors—perhaps an owner ultimately getting lured by a sweetheart deal in another city or engaging in some questionable management practices that alienated fans and caused them to justifiably withhold their support—but at the end of the day, the story of a lot of franchises, especially in the early years of sports leagues, involved them trying to find a place where they would be adequately supported. To find a home where that social contract—we try to win, you buy tickets—could be most successfully fulfilled.

But what happens if the teams don't hold up *their* end of the bargain? What if the people who own and operate them decide that winning is not particularly important to them? What if they find a way to circumvent the traditional incentives that are an essential part of that sports social contract and realize that they can make mountains of money even if the team is not particularly good? These are not theoretical questions. They describe a state of affairs that has emerged in sports in recent years and, if anything, is rapidly becoming the rule rather than the exception. And it's playing out in a number of ways.

Competition in the pursuit of victory is the very essence of sports. The entire enterprise, and that social contract I just mentioned, is premised on everyone involved attempting to win games. But the strategy of a great many professional sports teams in the past decade has been to ask, "What if we didn't try?"

Enter the concept of tanking: clubs intentionally fielding teams of players less talented than they could field in the hopes that by losing, they will (a) improve their draft position, thereby allowing them to, maybe, get better at some point in the future; and (b) save money in the process.

Tanking is a concept that was first and perhaps most notably observed in basketball. This makes sense, as basketball is a sport where one player can make an outsized difference in a team's future competitive prospects. The Houston Rockets of the 1983–84 season are considered "patient zero" in tanking studies, as they clearly punted the second half of their season that year in order to get into position to draft either Hakeem Olajuwon or Michael Jordan, both of whom became Hall of Famers. They got Olajuwon and later won two NBA titles with him. Their obvious efforts to lose in the second half of that season, however, led to the institution of the NBA draft lottery system the following year, which did not automatically give the top pick in the draft to the absolute worst team, thereby blunting the impulse to, essentially, throw a season in order to get a star player. But despite the lottery, which has been tweaked numerous times, the lure of some transformative amateur talent in upcoming drafts still incentivizes NBA teams to tank.

One of the more egregious examples of this came in an April 2006 game between the Minnesota Timberwolves and the Memphis Grizzlies that each team pretty clearly wanted to lose for different reasons. The Grizzlies, who were playoff bound, had an incentive to lose because obtaining a worse playoff seed would've given them a more favorable postseason matchup. The Timberwolves, meanwhile, had a strong incentive to lose because it would've ensured that they could keep a draft pick that they otherwise would have sent to the Los Angeles Clippers because of a recent trade. In order to hold on to that pick, Timberwolves coach Dwayne Casey allowed low-scoring, bench-warming post player Mark Madsen to chuck seven three-point attempts down the stretch of the game, all of which he missed. Casey was well aware of what he was doing too, saying afterward, "I hope what we did didn't make a mockery of the game." If you have to ask, Dwayne . . .

Perhaps the most famous recent example of NBA tanking was displayed by the Philadelphia 76ers of the mid-2010s. As the Sixers stockpiled players of very little value and traded away decent starters for injured players and payroll flexibility, management explicitly asked fans to "trust the process." It was a phrase clearly meant to tell fans that "we are losing on purpose and will continue to lose on purpose for some time, but there is a reason we are doing it." Philly lost a frightening number of games between 2013 and 2016 and were rewarded with high picks that allowed them to draft Ben Simmons and Joel Embiid, who formed the core of recent, more successful 76ers squads. The Sixers' tank job inspired others to copy them, with an arguable peak coming in the 2017–18 season when the

Dallas Mavericks, Memphis Grizzlies, Chicago Bulls, and Atlanta Hawks routinely threw out lineups that sometimes looked incapable of winning by design. There was no penalty imposed on any of those clubs for this strategy, but Dallas owner Mark Cuban was fined $600,000 after going on a podcast and admitting that for a number of reasons, his Mavericks were better off losing. Clearly, the lesson was that you can make a mockery of athletic competition, but you had better not admit to what you're doing.

The NFL, too, has had at least some isolated experience with tanking, specifically related to teams trying less than their best in an effort to draft a potential franchise quarterback. Back in 2011, fans of the Colts, Dolphins, Rams, and Vikings adopted the only partially tongue-in-cheek rallying cry, "Suck for Luck," referring to the coveted Stanford University quarterback Andrew Luck. In 2014, the Tampa Bay Buccaneers benched most of their starters in the final game of the season in order to ensure that they'd get top draft prospect Jameis Winston. Throughout the fall and early winter of 2019, the Cincinnati Bengals were drooling over the prospect of drafting LSU quarterback Joe Burrow and made on-field decisions that seemed specifically calculated to ensure that very possibility.

Baseball had been immune to the concept of tanking for most of its history for a number of reasons. The most prominent being that by the very nature of the sport, any one superstar baseball player is far less important to a team winning than any one superstar basketball player or any one NFL quarterback, thus making it silly for baseball teams to try to move up in draft position to get any one player. At the same time, baseball's draft has historically been more art than science, with far more seemingly "can't miss" players actually missing and far more superstars being drafted in later rounds than you'd ever see in basketball or football. At the same time, baseball's far more robust free agency system, as well as an international amateur free agency system, allowed teams to improve more quickly outside of the draft by spending big money for talent, thus diminishing the draft's importance and reducing the incentive to tank.

In more recent years, however, each and every one of the disincentives for baseball teams to tank has gone away, and multiple incentives for teams to tank have been created. For one thing, the notion that building a winner via the acquisition of amateur talent is difficult business was seemingly called into question by the Chicago Cubs and the Houston Astros of the late 2000s and early

2010s. Both of those clubs pursued an NBA-style tank, trading away what solid players they had on their rosters and willfully bottoming out to collect high draft picks. Within a few years of embarking on a tanking strategy, each of these teams won the World Series. The notion of rebuilding had always been present in baseball, but the idea of cutting it back to the bone like Houston and Chicago did, of being content to lose a boatload of games for a couple of seasons and then emerge as world-beaters caused the league to take notice and caused many to attempt to emulate them.

But there was more than just monkey see, monkey do at work. The structure of baseball, via the 2012 and 2016 collective bargaining agreements, greatly encouraged tanking and discouraged clubs from assuming a win-now approach involving the signing of free agents and otherwise making greater financial expenditures. Of note in this regard was the creation of a salary slotting system for the amateur draft in which a given draft pick would be paid no more than a predetermined bonus, with severe penalties on teams that exceeded slotted bonuses. This blunted the ability of draftees to make large bonus demands in an effort to scare off the teams with high picks, thereby allowing them to join winning teams who chose later in the draft. A couple of years after that, hard bonus caps were imposed in the international amateur free agent market too, curtailing a team's ability to make up for a poor draft position via the expenditure of big money on players from outside of the United States. In both the case of the draft and the international market, teams with worse records in the preceding system were allowed to spend the most money on young players. Finally, over the course of the last several collective bargaining agreements, concessions were won by management, which made the signing of free agents far less desirable, giving the draft an even greater significance thereby incentivizing losing as a means of future improvement.

The net result of all of this has been an epidemic of tanking in baseball. The basic tanking blueprint is as follows:

- Trade anyone of value on your major league roster for prospects;

- Save as much money as possible by using cheap players to fill out the roster;

- Stockpile high draft picks after your team loses a massive number of games for consecutive seasons and use those high draft picks to build an elite farm system;

- Allow prospects to develop in the minors while continuing to run out a lineup full of palookas; and

- When prospects are finally ready, bring them up in waves and win as many games as possible until they become expensive themselves.

While no team called what they were doing in this regard "tanking"—and while not every rebuilding process can fairly be called tanking—a lot of teams followed this blueprint, and it has led to a lot of bad baseball.

In both 2019 and 2021, four teams lost more than 100 games, tying a record. Nine other teams in those same years came close to hitting that dubious mark. Between 2018 and 2019, the Baltimore Orioles lost 223 games, giving them one of the worst two-year stretches in baseball history. After the pandemic-shortened 2020 season, they returned to a full schedule in 2021 and lost 110. The Tigers' 114 losses in 2019 was the fourth-most in baseball history and, but for the pandemic-shortened 2020 campaign, they would've stood a good chance of losing 100 again in 2020. All of this was merely the culmination of a several-years-long trend that also included the White Sox, the Blue Jays, the Marlins, the Royals, the Mariners, and the

Pirates. Other teams, while more superficially competitive for a time, have declined to improve themselves in the course of a given season, preferring to miss the postseason by many games than merely by a few.

As this has gone on, attendance across baseball has steadily declined for the past decade and a half after reaching a peak in 2007. In each of the five years before the pandemic, it went down. Fans, uninterested in watching games in which as much as a third of the league isn't interested in winning, are turning away.

"But wait!" you're thinking. "Didn't you say earlier that fans withdrawing support for losing teams is part of the sports social contract? Doesn't their doing so punish the teams who don't try to win, thereby encouraging them to change course and try harder lest they take it on the chin financially?" Well, you'd think so. But as more and more teams lose, and as attendance declines, revenues have continued to rise. Tanking has not hurt team owners' bottom line, either in baseball or in the other major sports. Mostly because teams are, increasingly, not really in the business of sports. At least not primarily.

In 2016, the Atlanta Braves lost their first nine games of the season. During a mid-April shareholders meeting, John Malone, the CEO of the company that owns the

Braves, was asked about the team's slow start. While previous Braves owner Ted Turner or the late New York Yankees owner George Steinbrenner may have groused in displeasure about losing teams on their watch, and may have fired managers or traded players in an effort to turn things around, Malone was unconcerned. It was not because he assumed the Braves would turn it around on their own—in any event, they would not, as they were en route to a ninety-three-loss season and a last place finish—but because he really didn't care. Why?

"Keep in mind," he told the assembled shareholders, "the Braves now are a fairly major real estate business as opposed to just a baseball club." And he was absolutely right about that.

As we discussed earlier, the primary reason the Braves moved to Truist Park in the city's northern suburbs was because it presented an opportunity for the club to develop the land around the new ballpark. They have done so via an entity called the Braves Development Company, which, based on the team's organizational chart, sits on equal footing with the team's baseball operations department, with both its head and the head of the baseball team reporting to team CEO Terry McGuirk. I follow the Braves closely, and I can tell you that when McGuirk speaks about how the Braves are doing—about whether they are "successful" and whether revenues are healthy—it's difficult to tell if he means the baseball team or the real estate business. I presume it's because, on a basic level, those things are nearly indistinguishable to the team. There is certainly tremendous overlap at least, given that in the years since the Braves moved to Truist Park, they have seen revenues increase dramatically, but a tremendous portion of those increased revenues have been plowed into building office buildings and hotels, from which the Braves no doubt expect to realize far greater returns in the long run than they might realize from winning a World Series.

The Braves are not alone in this. Similar developments have popped up in St. Louis, where Ballpark Village, a 150,000-square-foot mixed-use retail, entertainment, office, and residential district, has risen over the past decade. In Arlington, Texas, the Rangers' new ballpark is accompanied by a $250 million mixed-use development featuring restaurants and an outdoor event pavilion. The Boston Red Sox are redeveloping four parcels surrounding Fenway Park. In early 2023, the San Diego Padres and a handful of partners plan to break ground on a two-million-square-foot mixed-use development in downtown San Diego dubbed East Village Quarter, which represents a $1.4 billion investment. In 2020, the San Francisco Giants broke ground on the first phase of a $2.5 billion development called the Mission Rock project just across the inlet that forms the famous McCovey Cove next to Oracle Park and which will eventually feature ten buildings accommodating retail space, apartments, a parking garage, and a five-acre park. In Inglewood, California, the new stadium for the NFL's Los Angeles Rams and Los Angeles Chargers sits at the core of what is planned to be an $8 billion development project.

These sorts of developments are not rare, serendipitous opportunities taken advantage of by sports teams when they happen to arise. They are an inherent part of the new business model in sports, a model in which teams actively seek revenue streams that are not dependent upon winning games and are not imperiled by losing games. Potentially, the playing of games could even become a loss leader that will help the owners of these teams realize far more significant revenues than they ever could merely from selling tickets and TV broadcasting rights to a baseball or football team. Indeed, in 2021, when it was suggested that the Oakland Athletics, long in need of a new ballpark, simply build a new one on the seemingly ideal, transit-and-freeway-connected location of their current one, Major League Baseball commissioner Rob Manfred pushed back, saying that it is "not a viable option for the future vision of baseball." By this he did not mean that the site was not appropriate for the playing of baseball games. He meant that a ballpark on that location would take up acreage that the Athletics' owner, John Fisher, who also owns the land in question, would prefer to devote to the more lucrative business of retail, restaurant, condo, and office building development.

There's another major source of revenue sports teams and leagues are beginning to realize that, like real estate money, is not dependent upon who wins or who loses games: gambling.

This was all made possible on May 14, 2018, when the United States Supreme Court struck down a law that had outlawed sports gambling in every state except Nevada. The ruling began the spread of legalized sports gambling across the country, a process that, in reality, had already begun in anticipation of the ruling. Within days of the judgment being handed down, New Jersey had its sports gambling law on the books. Many other states quickly followed.

Early in the litigation which led to the Supreme Court paving the way for sports gambling, the major sports leagues actually took the side of the federal government in trying to keep the anti-gambling law on the books. There was an obvious reason for that: gambling and sports have, historically not mixed with the specter of the fixed baseball games of the early twentieth century, mob-backed point-shaving scandals in college basketball in the 1980s, and a referee-led game-fixing scandal being uncovered in the NBA in 2007—all of which loomed large in the mind of every sports executive. However, when it became likely that the states challenging the law would win the case, the leagues switched sides and joined the plaintiffs in the suit. They saw the writing on the wall and would make sure that if there was going to be legal sports gambling in this country, they would get a piece of the action.

Initially, various leagues weren't quite sure how to do it. Baseball's first stab at it was to attempt to be like a shovel salesman during the Gold Rush, standing by and providing the newly emerging state sports gambling authorities the rights to their intellectual property, statistics, and logos that would inevitably be used in the marketing and administration of gambling products. When the states basically ignored MLB's claim that they should get a cut on such grounds, they and the rest of the major sports leagues changed tactics and began to partner up with casinos directly. In late November 2018, MGM Resorts became the first ever "Official Gaming Partner of Major League Baseball." Since then, multiple teams have cut individual deals with both brick-and-mortar casinos and online companies like DraftKings and FanDuel. As have the major sports media companies like ESPN, the Athletic, Fox Sports, CBS Sports, NBC Sports, and Turner Sports. Sixteen current MLB clubs, seventeen NBA teams, and fourteen NHL teams are currently broadcast on regional sports networks affiliated with and named after the Bally's Corporation.

As a part of these affiliations, gambling has moved front and center in the promotion of professional sports, and it goes way, way beyond the almost quaint sight of seeing casinos and casino-owned resorts advertising during games. MGM, for example, has been given access to MLB's official statistics for its online and casino-based sports books and is allowed to see each game's lineups before they are released to the public so they can set betting odds. MGM is also given some so-called "enhanced" proprietary statistics on an exclusive basis, which help it to more efficiently rake in gamblers' money. Beyond all of that, multiple teams have begun running sports books inside their stadiums and arenas, and all of the league-partnered sports networks have ratcheted up gambling-specific content on their broadcasts.

These sorts of arrangements, which have become ubiquitous in sports over the past four years, allow sports leagues and teams to make a substantial amount of money. Unlike the actual playing of games, this money is made no matter the outcome because (a) the house always wins; and (b) sports teams and leagues are increasingly *becoming* the house.

———————

Another way in which team owners are making it so that winning and losing is less important to their bottom line is by taking ownership, in a sense, of their entire sport in a way that makes them all winners, even if their own particular team is a loser.

Since 2015, Major League Baseball has embarked on a grand vision to unify baseball, and softball for that matter, at all levels under the Major League Baseball banner. The idea is to integrate minor league baseball, independent professional leagues, and amateur baseball stakeholders into a single organizational structure under MLB's control. The concept, referred to as "One Baseball," has, to date, been talked about by the league and its leaders as being rooted in a desire to improve the league's on-field product by streamlining player development and to get more kids playing baseball, thus enhancing the talent pipeline. And it may very well do that, but there are obvious financial incentives at play here too in terms of developing the next generation of baseball fans and realizing other longer-term financial returns.

In this, it's not entirely unlike FIFA's governance structure in soccer, in which various interrelated leagues across multiple levels sit under a single organizational umbrella. Like FIFA, of course, those under that umbrella who possess the most clout—in this case Major League Baseball and its thirty owners—will obviously benefit the most. In baseball's case, it will benefit via its greater control over the minor leagues, which Major League Baseball has radically contracted and realigned in a way that cuts development costs and turns teams that may have been competing with MLB clubs for fans' entertainment dollars into, basically, junior partners. It also gives MLB control over what were once independent leagues and what was once a collective of independent private, for-profit development venues for amateur talent, such as prospect showcases and tournaments. Through One Baseball, MLB is also investing in elite amateur baseball infrastructure abroad, focusing efforts in talent-rich Latin American countries such as Venezuela, Colombia, Panama, Curaçao, and Aruba. All of this top-down control over the player development pipeline likewise allows it to reduce the size of the MLB draft, limiting the number of players who can command large bonuses as drafted talent and making them scramble for fewer jobs on fewer minor league clubs. The One Baseball initiative may very well create greater efficiencies in the overall structure of baseball, but it's aimed at giving teams greater control over costs and a greater share of the overall revenues the sport at large creates. In so doing, every single owner has less to lose if, in a given year or five, his own team loses some games or loses some money.

A similar dynamic took place earlier this century when Major League Baseball founded the streaming media platform MLB Advanced Media, which was originally intended for the digital dissemination of baseball games but was actually spun off into a company called BAMTech and then sold to Disney for several billion dollars. Similarly, Major League Soccer has a marketing business called Soccer United Marketing that is jointly owned by the league's team owners, with MLS commissioner Don Garber serving as its top executive. Soccer United Marketing provides a significant revenue source that is not at all dependent upon those owners' teams winning games and pleasing fans. The NFL, NBA, and NHL all have such businesses and initiatives as well.

Sports is a business, and there is nothing wrong with the owners of a business exploiting new sources of revenue beyond just the games themselves. But there are some big-picture ideas that should be pretty obvious when thinking about the business of sports, and one of them is that social contract I mentioned at the outset of this chapter. The better the game in terms of competitiveness, excitement, and entertainment value, the better it is for the sport. The more fans who want to watch your games, the better it is for the sport.

What we're seeing more and more of lately, however, is a disconnect between those good things—competitive excitement and fan interest—and revenue. Indeed, there is less of a connection between those things than ever before. There is an increasing gap between the revenue that sports teams and leagues make from the playing of games and what they make from non-game sources such as real estate development, gambling and tech initiatives, and marketing side deals. A greater share of the money going into the pockets of team owners is coming from sources independent of what happens on the field with any of their specific teams. It's not money gained from winning games or attracting fans.

Even TV money—sports' most important source of income that, obviously, is directly related to the playing of games—invokes this problem, thanks to the structure most of the broadcasting deals have taken on in recent years. Cable companies, desperate for the steady, prestigious, DVR-proof and cord-cutting-resistant product that is professional sports—have given out ten-, twenty-, and even thirty-year broadcast deals to various teams and leagues. They're paying teams and leagues billions of guaranteed dollars for those broadcast rights, and over time frames as long as those, there is no way to guarantee that teams will work to be competitive on a consistent basis. There exists no real incentive for teams to spend money on players and make themselves competitive in the way they would have to if the next TV deal was always just a couple of years away.

If you own a team and you are getting guaranteed billions from TV over the next couple of decades, billions from your park-adjacent real estate development, and billions in random windfalls from gambling and internet side businesses, why put any money into your team at all? Why pay to sign the best players? Why try particularly hard to compete? In the past, when winning games and drawing fans was pretty important, you had an incentive to field a respectable team as often as possible lest your fans abandon you, but where's that incentive now? As evidenced by how little sports revenues have been harmed by the tanking epidemic, there's a pretty good argument that, actually, there isn't much of one at all.

6
BALLS AND STRIKES

August 11, 1994, was a pretty typical Thursday in Major League Baseball as far as the schedule went. Eighteen of baseball's twenty-eight teams were in action, with the other ten getting the day off before what would normally be a full slate of fourteen games. But on Friday, there were no games at all. There would be none for the rest of the season, in fact, with nearly 950 regular season games canceled along with the playoffs and World Series—all because of the 1994–95 Major League Baseball strike.

If you were old enough to remember that time, and if you were paying at least a little attention, you probably remember the players being held responsible for the cancellation of the season and the World Series. In a Gallup poll taken at the time, fans favored the owners over the players, with a plurality of fans taking management's side. This polling reflected general dispositions, seeing as subjects were almost never told the specific details of either side's position. It was a default favoring of team ownership over the players.

On a basic level, this was understandable. The players were the ones who were going on strike, right? They were the greedy millionaires who wanted more money to play a kids' game than any of the rest of us would see in our lifetimes, the story went, so why were they striking anyway? The owners claimed they were going broke paying them all of those millions, and all they wanted was some payroll control in the form of a salary cap, just like football and basketball had. Those sports were thriving; if it worked there, why wouldn't it work in baseball? Why ruin what had been a wonderful, historic season to date with a work stoppage? Why take away my Yankees or my Dodgers or my Cubs?

If only it were so simple. If only it were about the players and the owners not seeing eye-to-eye on a competing set of proposals in a given round of negotiations. Then, perhaps, a strike could have been easily averted. The 1994–95 baseball strike, however, was about far more than that. It was the culmination of nearly thirty years of acrimony between the players and the owners, fueled by distrust, deceit, and resentment. Thirty years that had already seen numerous skirmishes and at least one protracted battle between the sides but that broke out into full-scale war in August 1994. And before those thirty years? A century's worth of domination of the players by the owners that stands comparable, at least in form if not in substance, to any number of other labor stories in our nation's history. Stories in which those who owned the businesses and raked in the millions and, eventually, billions from the labor of their workers refused to share it equitably with those workers, refused to create working conditions which were fair and, in some cases, humane, and refused to negotiate about any of it in good faith.

It's hard to look at today's professional sports landscape—one in which athletes are fabulously wealthy celebrities living profoundly privileged lifestyles—and appreciate that not too long ago, their predecessors as sports superstars were treated like pieces of property. They had no pensions, no healthcare benefits, and their salaries were such that most of them had to take regular jobs in the off-season to make ends meet. The change from that state of affairs to the one that prevails today was not something that took place a century ago. Most of it took place since the 1960s due to athletes like the ballplayers who went on strike in 1994 standing up to the leagues and owners and demanding a fair share of the revenue that their talent and celebrity provided. Due to players, through their unions, demanding working conditions that acknowledged that they were employees deserving of humane treatment, not gladiators who could be discarded the moment their bodies became broken and their utility as a drawing card came to an end.

Baseball's labor history is a bit more extensive, and because of the sheer amount of acrimony and litigation, its transformation from a sport in which the players were at the mercy of the owners to one in which they exercised some labor muscle has been better chronicled than that of the other major sports. Still, the pattern it followed is not unlike that which we've seen elsewhere. And it's a history that once you become better acquainted with it, should make you think a bit differently about player-owner disputes when they arise.

———————

For most of the entire first century of professional baseball's existence, baseball's owners controlled basically everything. In the first decade or two of professional baseball, players freely shopped their services around and made pretty decent money for the day. But in the 1880s, the owners inserted a clause in every single player's contract that came to be known as the reserve clause, which in 1887, *Lippincott's Magazine* described as being used as, "a handle for the manipulation of a traffic in players, a sort of speculation in livestock, by which they are bought, sold and transferred like so many sheep."

The reserve clause gave teams rights to a player's services in perpetuity—automatically renewing their contract for another year when the previous term ended and doing so at whatever salary the owners saw fit to pay. The reserve clause sapped players of any control they had over their professional lives. Owners dictated if players played, where players played, and how much money the players made. If they didn't like it, they could go get a job in a factory or something. Their baseball lives would be dictated by the men who owned the teams.

The players mounted a few efforts at unionization in the years that followed, but nothing really came of it. In 1885, they created the Brotherhood of Professional Baseball players, the first serious effort to organize a labor union for athletes of any kind, in an effort to increase their salaries and, most importantly, end the reserve clause. The organization gained official recognition by the National League, but owners were almost completely unwilling to make significant concessions, and the players were unwilling to strike. That led, in 1890, to the players starting a competing league in which they owned the teams themselves. The aptly-named Players League, however, lasted only one season before collapsing, with the players skulking back to the National League. It would be a half century before even modest efforts were made to improve ballplayers' labor lot.

In the 1940s, in response to some rudimentary, abortive efforts to unionize by the players, the owners agreed to set up a pension system, but it was woefully underfunded. The players finally formed a real union in 1953: the Major League Baseball Players Association, or the MLBPA. It was, however, about as weak as a union could be. This was primarily because its top nonplayer official, a labor lawyer named Jonas Normal Lewis, was personally opposed to the notion of workers going on strike as a matter of principl, and he sharply advised the players to never threaten to do so. It's also worth noting that his feelings on that may have been influenced by the fact that he worked for the same law firm that represented the owners of the New York Giants, which was a conflict of interest to say the least.

It probably wouldn't have made much of a difference if Lewis wasn't conflicted because the players simply didn't seem all that interested in actually behaving as unionized workers. They and their predecessors had been subjected to an extraordinarily successful, century-long, owner-led propaganda campaign that had convinced them they played a game for a living rather than worked in a profession. They also, like everyone else in the country, had been impacted by the larger anti-union sentiment, which is frequently prevalent in American society. In light of that, Lewis's "strikes are bad!" advice was something most players took to heart. Unions, your average ballplayer of the 1950s and early 1960s thought, meant the mob and corruption and ugly strikes would cost players paychecks, and they didn't want any part of that.

By 1966, the players' concerns about the pension being underfunded resurfaced. This time, their fears of what a strong union meant notwithstanding, they decided to fire Lewis and hire a full-time, independent union chief. The man they voted for was one John Robert Cannon. Cannon, like Lewis, was an anti-strike guy. On top of that, he was openly lobbying for the job of commissioner of Major League Baseball, which was an even greater conflict of interest than Lewis's. Cannon asked for too much money after being offered the job, however, so the players went with their second choice: an economist with the United Steelworkers Union named Marvin Miller who agreed to a lower salary and thus got the job.

Miller changed everything when it came to the labor dynamics of Major League Baseball. Entire books can be—and have been—written about his tenure, but here are the highlights:

- As soon as Miller took office in 1966, he renegotiated the pension plan in such a way that not only increased its value to players but which, due to (a) his pointing out that the owners had illegally withdrawn money from it in the past; and (b) the owners making ridiculous lowball offers before caving, galvanized the support of the once-disinterested union membership;

- In 1968, Miller negotiated the first collective bargaining agreement (CBA), which won the players a 42 percent increase in minimum salary and written procedures for the arbitration of player grievances before the commissioner. The next CBA, in 1970, gave the players even greater grievance arbitration rights, establishing neutral three-arbitrator panels rather than hearings before the commissioner. This would prove to be extraordinarily significant in just a few short years;

- From 1969 to 1972, player Curt Flood mounted a legal challenge against the reserve clause, objecting to his being traded by the Cardinals to the Phillies and demanding that he be allowed, like any other worker, to choose where he worked. While Flood ultimately lost that case after taking it all the way to the US Supreme Court, his challenge—and Miller's support of that challenge—emboldened other players to challenge the reserve clause;

- At the beginning of the 1972 season, Miller led the MLBPA on a twelve-day strike—the first strike in the history of Major League Baseball—over pension payments and in an effort to obtain salary arbitration. The players won on both counts. They now knew the power of collective action and would be less wary of using it in the future;

- In 1974, Oakland A's star pitcher Catfish Hunter used the arbitration procedure Miller had obtained for the players to challenge A's owner Charlie Finley's failure to make a contractually obligated annuity payment. Hunter won, and because Finley had breached the contract, it was torn up. Hunter became baseball's first star player to be able to pick which club he played for in nearly a century. He signed with the Yankees for a then-enormous five years and $3.5 million with a $1 million signing bonus. If the players doubted the value of free agency, they knew it now; and

• Later that year, Miller convinced two pitchers—Andy Messersmith of the Los Angeles Dodgers and Dave McNally of the Baltimore Orioles—to play out their contracts and not sign new ones, after which they sought an arbitration ruling that they were, in fact, free agents, and that the automatic renewal provision of the reserve clause was illegal. In 1975, they won, which ended the reserve clause and ushered in the era of free agency in sports.

During Miller's tenure as the executive director of the MLBPA, pensions were fully funded, per diems were dramatically increased, free agency was achieved, and players' average annual salary rose from $19,000 in 1966 to $326,000 in 1982. There had been no run of success like that in the history of sports labor. Many, in fact, have argued that Miller made the MLBPA the most powerful and successful union in the country, bar none. In the twenty years after Miller's departure as the head of the union, the owners attempted to claw back the gains players had made as a result of his work, culminating in that 1994–95 strike, which was forced not by greedy players seeking even more money than they already made, but by the efforts of then-acting MLB commissioner Bud Selig and a handful of like-minded owners who were hell-bent on breaking the union.

The union history of the other major sports broadly tracks that of baseball's. In 1955, Tim Horton, the star defenseman for the Toronto Maple Leafs and namesake of the coffee and donut franchise, broke his leg in a game, wasn't paid for the time he missed, and had his salary cut the following year, with the team citing his decrease in effectiveness. The treatment of Horton, who worked a construction job in the off-season to make ends meet, was not uncommon. It inspired Ted Lindsay of the Detroit Red Wings to attempt to rally players to form a union during the late 1950s. The Red Wings promptly traded Lindsay to Chicago in an effort to cripple the nascent unionization drive. Other hockey union organizers would get traded or demoted to the minor leagues solely because they were gaining traction in organizing. It wasn't until a decade after Lindsay's efforts began that enough players had banded together to convince the owners to recognize the National Hockey League Players Association. As in baseball, the NHL players were forced to go on strike on a number of occasions in order to secure and consolidate early gains. They went on a short strike in 1992, a longer strike in 1994, and were subjected to an owner-imposed lockout in 2004, which cost the entire season.

In basketball, there was no pension plan, no per diems, no minimum wage, and no healthcare benefits before efforts at unionization began to take hold in the mid-to-late 1950s. The average player salary was $8,000. Then, the league's top player, Bob Cousy, organized players who collectively threatened to pull out of the 1955 All-Star game if the owners did not agree to sit down and bargain with players over issues like limiting the number of unpaid exhibition games and being paid for promotional appearances. The walkout was averted, but it was not until two years later, when Cousy and the players threatened to strike, that the union was officially recognized. Early victories for the union included a $7 per diem, moving expenses for players who were traded midseason, and a bigger cut of playoff revenues. There have been a number of labor actions in basketball too, most notably in 1998 when the NBA owners locked out the players, costing over a third of the season.

In the NFL, where the physical toll of the sport and the comparatively short careers of its players make workplace conditions and health and safety concerns paramount, unionization likewise began in the mid-1950s. At the time, players were not paid for up to eight weeks of training camp and exhibition games during which they were just as likely to be hurt and to miss time and lose out on future pay as they would be in the regular season. In 1956, players on the Green Bay Packers and Cleveland Browns formed a union and successfully forced the league to address many of their grievances, as well as establish an official minimum salary and a pension plan. Still, the National Football League Players Association was not recognized by the NFL as the official bargaining agent for the players until 1968, when its first CBA was signed. NFL players went on strike in September 1982 in search of baseball-style free agency and a larger cut of broadcast revenue. They were only partially successful in that regard, and the strike ended after seven weeks' worth of games had been canceled. They went on strike again in 1987, but fewer games were lost because the owners hired non-union scabs to play in their place. In 2011, the owners locked out the players for an eighteen-week period during the off-season that shut down the free agent signing period and training camp and kept players from seeing team doctors, entering or working out at team facilities, or communicating with coaches.

As a result of athletes unionizing and, subsequently, going on strike or withstanding lockouts, their lot has dramatically improved. Athletes have, however, seen diminishing returns over time, especially compared to the massive revenue increases team owners have realized, and their share of their sports' revenues is now lower, proportionately speaking, than it was back in the 1990s. This is mostly because owners have changed tactics. Rather than trying to crush the unions and impose salary controls in one fell swoop, they have slowly chipped away at the gains achieved by the players. And they've done a very good job of it.

In baseball, they have done so by instituting a revenue sharing system and a robust "luxury tax" that penalizes teams for going over certain payroll levels, which discourages spending on salaries while not, at least nominally, changing the deal for players. They have likewise imposed a number of restrictions on what can be spent on draftees and international amateur free agents, neither of whom are represented by the union. They have similarly made it a priority to pay as little as possible to minor league players, going so far as to lobby Congress to classify minor league ballplayers as "seasonal employees" for labor law purposes, allowing them to be paid sub-minimum-wage salaries. All of these moves against lower-paid, nonunionized players trickle up, as it were, to the major league level, where increasingly desperate young players find themselves more eager to sign team-friendly deals early in their careers rather than hold out until they can exercise greater bargaining power as veterans. There is a clear sense in baseball that many teams would rather save money on player salaries than win games. Indeed, until 2019, Major League Baseball gave out an actual championship belt to the executives of the franchise that paid the least amount to players in salary arbitration proceedings. The practice, which had been a secret among MLB executives, ceased after it was publicly reported.

A similar dynamic exists in football, where the latest collective bargaining agreement increased the regular-season schedule from sixteen to seventeen games. While the agreement also called for an increase in the player's take of overall revenue from 47 to 48.5 percent, that represented a 3.1 percent revenue increase for a 6.3 percent increase in games played. The new agreement likewise took a bye week out of the schedule, leaving players to play seventeen games in an eighteen-week span, despite the lip service the league pays to concerns about the health and safety of players. As for that health and safety, the NFL has come quite a long way in acknowledging and addressing the health crisis brought on by concussions and both short-term and long-term brain injuries as a result of the inherent violence of the sport—which in the early 1990s former commissioner Paul Tagliabue dismissed as a phony, journalist-created issue—but even with an increasingly stringent set of concussion protocols, teams continue to send injured players out onto the field, putting them at risk of serious health consequences.

Labor disputes in sports tend to be discounted as pointless, distracting battles between millionaires and billionaires, but the fact remains that the playing of sports is labor and athletes are workers. Their jobs exist because we, as fans, have created an economy that supports and rewards them. Yes, the athletes earn salaries ranging from the hundreds of thousands to tens of millions of dollars annually, but they are nonetheless unionized workers whose interests stand in opposition to those of the billionaires and corporate conglomerates that sign their checks. Billionaires and corporations who make enormous profits off the players through TV revenue, ticket sales, and all manner of ancillary revenue streams.

So often we hear complaints about how much players are paid, but rarely do we hear complaints about how much revenue the owners, who willingly pay them this money, rake in. Rarely do those who take issue with how much money players make appreciate that, if the players made less, the savings would not go into reduced ticket prices or reduced beer prices. Rather, that money, like all money that is not spent on salaries or the infrastructure of sports—stadiums, front office employees, equipment, and training, etc.—is money that goes directly into the owners' pocket.

In the greater business world, we tend not to take the side of companies that lay off workers, pay below-market salaries, fail to provide medical benefits, and pocket massive revenues, but as sports fans, we do it pretty consistently. A lot of that has to do with the fact that, in sports, unlike in business, the so-called little guy is making millions. And a lot of that has to do with the fact that in sports, unlike in business, we have an affinity and an allegiance to the company because it is the keeper of the uniforms and the logos and a history in which we are personally and emotionally invested.

We as fans should be mindful of the ways in which the billionaires who run professional sports leverage our allegiances and our emotions to benefit them when they enter into negotiations with players over salaries and working conditions. We should resist falling into the trap of dismissing these battles as meaningless or supporting management's side of those battles. We should eschew the sentiment that almost always prevails whenever the business of labor relations threatens to interfere with the playing of games in which fans ask why professional athletes—men who are paid millions to play a game— should be paid even more.

When I was a kid, I never rushed down to the corner store to buy a pack of owner trading cards. I have never purchased a team jersey that had the owner's name on the back of it. I don't root for owners during the games; I root for the players. I don't see any reason why I should stop doing that when the competition leaves the field and moves to the negotiating table.

7
HOMETOWN HEROES

In October 2014, I was in Kansas City, covering the World Series between the Royals and the San Francisco Giants. A few hours before game time, a Royals' media relations staffer handed me a sheet of paper with all of that day's pregame activities and events. The World Series is a best-of-seven games affair, and in 2014, it did indeed go a full seven games. The items on the list, however, were just the events for Game 1:

- COMMISSIONER SELIG'S VISIT WITH LOCAL VETERANS: The day of special activities designed to honor veterans will begin with Baseball Commissioner Allan H. (Bud) Selig visiting local veterans at the Kansas City VA Medical Center Honor Annex. He will be joined by MLB Chief Operating Officer Rob Manfred, David and Dan Glass (Royals Chief Executive Officer and President, respectively), Royals Legend John Mayberry, the United States Secretary of Veterans Affairs Robert A. McDonald and Vice Chairman of the Joint Chiefs of Staff Admiral James A. Winnefeld.

- PRE-GAME CEREMONY AND CEREMONIAL FIRST PITCH FEATURING LOCAL VETERAN: A special pre-game ceremony will feature Secretary Robert A. McDonald and Admiral James A. Winnefeld, who is the Nation's second highest ranking military officer, along with Staff Sergeant Pedro Sotelo (disabled and separated from service).

- Singing "God Bless America" before the bottom of the 7th inning will be Retired Naval Petty Officer 1st Class Generald Wilson.

- NEW WBV PSAs ON GAME ONE FOX TELECAST: Major League Baseball will unveil two new public service announcements (PSAs) in support of Welcome Back Veterans. The spots capture both the emotional spirit and significance of baseball's unique role in welcoming back our service men and women. The creative and production of both spots were handled by BarrettSF.

- BANK OF AMERICA SUPPORT: Bank of America, the Official Bank of Major League Baseball, will provide American flags for fans at each Kauffman Stadium entrance, and ask those in attendance to participate in a "Stand and Salute" moment during the 7th inning stretch, immediately following "God Bless America," to honor service members and veterans. This moment will culminate the bank's efforts to capture one million expressions of thanks for members of the military in 2014 as part of its "Express Your Thanks" campaign.

- BUDWEISER OUR HERO SEATS: Former U.S. Senator Bob Dole, the pride of Russell, Kansas, who served in the U.S. Army during World War II as a combat infantryman, will be honored in the Budweiser Our Hero Seat. After suffering serious injuries, Dole studied law and went on to serve in the Kansas Statehouse and later the U.S. Congress for more than 35 years. Dole has donated his actual seats to SSGT Matthew Gonzales, of Raytown, Missouri, who served in the U.S. Army for nine years, and is now battling a rare and aggressive service-related cancer that developed during a deployment to Iraq 2007.

- BUCK O'NEIL LEGACY SEAT: Continuing the Royals tradition of honoring a member of the community who embodies an aspect of the spirit of the former Negro Leagues Baseball player, U.S. Marine Corps Veteran Tony Clark will sit in the Buck O'Neil Legacy Seat. The Augusta, Kansas native Clark now uses his experience in the battlefield to run ultra-marathons and marathons in his efforts to raise awareness and funds for several military and Veteran causes.

- "PLAY BALL!": Austin Sides, the son of United States Air Force Major Robert Sides (both of whom were featured in the WBV—Royals Surprise PSA), will yell "Play Ball!" before the start of Game One.

I was an adult on 9/11, and I had lived in post-9/11 America for thirteen years by the time this press release was handed to me. I fully understood what had happened to the country and its culture in that time. I understood that the tributes to the military and everything related to 9/11 and the wars that soon began to rage in its wake took place at things like ball games, concerts, awards ceremonies, and other public events because the nation was in need of a coming together, and those are the sorts of places where people come together. Given this understandable nexus between the need of the nation to express these feelings and those places of national convergence, I understood why people made a big deal about President George W. Bush throwing out the first pitch at the first game after 9/11 and why ESPN produced a dramatic documentary about the event. I understood why baseball teams took to wearing uniforms with camouflage and why police officers and firefighters were honored at games. I understood why giant American flags were unfurled in outfields and why warplanes flew overhead just as the singer hit "*and the home of the brave*" in the national anthem.

But sitting there in that press box that afternoon, it struck me just how *de rigueur* and corporate-sponsored this sort of patriotic display had become. And how, more than a decade after 9/11, and after the initial, genuine need for national convergence had ceased, we were still doing this, as if it were the morning of September 12, 2001. We were doing it despite the fact that real divisions about the country's post-9/11 course, its political decisions, and its decisions about the waging of war had created a considerable rift in the nation as a whole.

That day, in the World Series press box, I wrote an article in which I said that "however well-intentioned

MLB's military and veteran-related initiatives are, at some point over the past 13 years they have become rote at best, overblown and exploited by corporate interests at worst, and maybe it's time to dial it back a bit." But then, less than a year later, we learned that not all of these gestures were even well-intentioned. Indeed, they were part of a full-blown, federally funded propaganda campaign.

In the fall of 2015, Senators John McCain and Jeff Flake released an oversight report, which revealed that the Pentagon had spent nearly $7 million over the previous few years to pay for patriotic displays during NFL, MLB, NBA, NHL, and MLS games and at NASCAR and IndyCar races. The purpose, as admitted to by Department of Defense spokespersons, was to serve as a recruiting tool. From the report:

> These paid tributes included on-field color guard, enlistment and reenlistment ceremonies, performances of the national anthem, full-field flag details, ceremonial first pitches and puck drops. The National Guard paid teams for the "opportunity" to sponsor military appreciation nights and to recognize its birthday. It paid the Buffalo Bills to sponsor its Salute to the Service game. DOD even

paid teams for the "opportunity" to perform surprise welcome home promotions for troops returning from deployments and to recognize wounded warriors. . . . It is hard to understand how a team accepting taxpayer funds to sponsor a military appreciation game, or to recognize wounded warriors or returning troops, can be construed as anything other than paid patriotism.

In a statement accompanying the report, Senators McCain and Flake noted that ceremonies honoring troops at professional sporting events, "are not actually being conducted out of a sense of patriotism, but for profit in the form of millions in taxpayer dollars going from the Department of Defense to wealthy pro sports franchises. . . . Fans should have confidence that their hometown heroes are being honored because of their honorable military service, not as a marketing ploy."

But a marketing ploy it was, with NFL teams receiving the majority of the paid patriotism money. As far as specific teams, the Atlanta Falcons led the way, receiving $879,000, which included underwriting for an event in 2013 during which a roaring crowd cheered as the Falcons welcomed eighty National Guard members onto the field to unfurl a giant American flag. The New England Patriots who, given their name, one would assume wouldn't need to be paid for such things, accepted $700,000 in exchange for patriotic displays. The Buffalo Bills got $650,000. The Atlanta Braves received $450,000, which was the most of any Major League Baseball team. The Wisconsin Air National Guard had actually paid the Milwaukee Brewers for Sunday performances of "God Bless America" in 2014. The Minnesota Wild were paid the most among NHL teams at $570,000.

This kind of propaganda was galling and manipulative, as fans were clearly led to believe that the ubiquitous salutes to the troops, "Hometown Hero" tribute, and even renditions of "God Bless America" were public services by the team or, possibly, spontaneous tributes. The revelation that it was bought and paid for served to cheapen genuine patriotism. The government used sports to manipulate public sentiment about the military, patriotism, and sports teams, and leagues gladly accepted money and allowed them to do it.

Congress put an end to paid patriotism after the McCain/Flake report came out, but military glorification remains big business for professional sports.

Each year, Major League Baseball puts its players in military-themed caps and jerseys on multiple occasions and then sells replicas of those caps and jerseys to the public. Fighter jet flyovers still take place before NFL games. Before the men's final of the 2017 US Open tennis tournament, a Marine Corps color guard joined West Point cadets in a ceremony to remember the victims of 9/11, displayed an oversized American flag, and gave a performance of "God Bless America," after which there was a flyover of four US fighter jets. It's unclear if the two finalists in that match, who were from Spain and South Africa, were appropriately moved. Whatever they made of it, they could not have escaped the conclusion that the union of the military with spectator sports in this country is strong and perhaps unbreakable.

William Astore, a retired United States Air Force colonel and history professor, was at that US Open and wrote about it for the *Huffington Post* the following year. The windup to that article hits at the disconnect inherent in that bond:

> Driven by corporate agendas and featuring exaggerated military displays, mass-spectator sports are helping to shape what Americans perceive and

believe. In stadiums across the nation, on screens held in our hands or dominating our living rooms, we witness fine young men and women in uniform unfurling massive flags on football fields and baseball diamonds, even on tennis courts, as combat jets scream overhead. . . . But let's be clear: this is not what war is all about. War is horrific. War features the worst of the human condition. When we blur sports and the military, adding corporate agendas into the mix, we're not just doing a disservice to our troops and our athletes; we're doing a disservice to ourselves. We're weakening the integrity of democracy in America.

Howard Bryant, an author and a senior writer for ESPN, extensively catalogued this conflation of sports, patriotism, and militarism in his 2018 book *The Heritage: Black Athletes, a Divided America, and the Politics of Patriotism.* He he noted that even in the post-paid-patriotism era, the tributes and the displays to the military have continued and, if anything, have expanded. Now, instead of being solely dedicated to the armed forces, there is an increasing inclusion of the police, firefighters, and other first responders in these tributes. Sports teams, leagues, and their broadcast partners never hesitate to highlight troops or cops in uniform when they're spotted in a stadium, be they there as fans or working at the game as part of an official event. Authority, as defined by our armed forces and police forces, continues to play a big part in the selling of sports to America. And sports play a big part in selling authority to America.

And it's not likely to go away any time soon. Here's Bryant, writing for ESPN in 2013, with words that were still relevant when his book came out five years later and which remain relevant now, nearly a decade later:

The old conventions of sports leagues and fans coming to the ballpark to escape the problems of the world disappeared when the towers fell. Sports, which were once by demand of the paying customers and the league themselves a neutral oasis from a dangerous world, have since become the epicenter of community and national exhalation. The ballpark, in the time of two murky wars and a constant threat of international and domestic terrorism, has been for the last dozen years a place for patriotism. The industry that once avoided the complex world now embraces it, serving as the chief staging ground for expressions of patriotism, and has codified it into game-day identity.

A dynamic that was supposed to be temporary has become permanent.

Sports teams and leagues have leveraged our loyalty for financial gain. For advantages in labor negotiations. To obtain favorable treatment from state and local governments. For the past two decades, sports has been the vehicle for a different sort of fan manipulation. Political manipulation, in service of an agenda that is performatively patriotic and shamelessly militaristic. As sports fans, it is incumbent upon us to ask whether we want to be a part of that. It is incumbent upon us to ask, if we do not want to be a part of that, and if we do not wish to walk away from sports altogether, how we can reconcile our fandom for the games we love with the manner in which the leagues and teams which sanction those games behave? To ask whether we can carve out a fandom that is not defined by adherence to the messages those teams and leagues author because, as we have seen, those messages are often at odds with our own priorities.

To this point, we have observed how sports are run by a sports-industrial complex that quite often isn't all that interested in sports for the same reasons we are and that certainly does not always have our best interests in mind. Now, we must ask, as sports fans, what we are supposed to do about that?

Often, when I pose questions about a given act of the sports-industrial complex to sports fans, I'm met with rationalization or emotional defenses born of that sort of fandom that is akin to the political tribalism I mentioned back in the first chapter. With attempts to isolate wrongdoers as a single team, or a single owner, or a single league, while rushing to claim that their behavior does not reflect more broadly than that. "Yes, the Cincinnati Bengals' stadium deal is terrible, but the one proposed for my Oakland A's is necessary!" Or maybe I hear some good old-fashioned whataboutism, in which one team's transgression in the past means that one need not dwell on the more recent transgression in one's own backyard. "It was shameful how the Sixers tanked five years ago, but my Pistons are simply being smart." Denial is always available too. Indeed, denial is commonly practiced by sports fans in lower-leverage situations—"We didn't get beat because they're better than us, we just had a bad day!"—so why wouldn't it be practiced when the stakes are higher? "The Braves' move to Cobb County isn't about race or money. They simply moved to where the fans were."

All of these approaches are, in the end, self-defeating. They play into the hands of the sports-industrial complex by turning what they do off the field into mere extensions of what they do on the field. It turns it all into a game in which, really, who's to say what's right and what's wrong? We all just have opinions!

In an ideal world, fans would band together to fight the sports-industrial complex and use their collective power to bend it toward better, more fan-friendly ends. I'm not so naive, however, to think that's realistic. Mostly because it's basically never happened. Even the most often-cited example doesn't actually apply. It came in the wake of the creation of the so-called Super League in which, in 2021, twenty elite European soccer clubs stood poised to form a breakaway confederation only to see the effort immediately and stunningly collapse in the space of forty-eight hours as angry fans took to the streets. That anger was genuine, and those protesting fans made for great visuals, but if it was just marching fans, the Super League likely would've gone on.

No, the real reason for the effort's collapse was the pressure applied by governing bodies such as FIFA and the

English, German, Italian, French, and Spanish domestic leagues and non-Super League clubs, which made it clear to the would-be Super League participants that breaking away would be bad for them. The worst impulses of the sports-industrial complex can be halted by a civil war, the example of the Super League showed, but there is nothing to suggest that fans directly taking on the sports-industrial complex is anything other than a doomed exercise in asymmetric warfare. In the end, the sports-industrial complex is going to do what it wants.

What it cannot do, however, is force you to go along with it. It cannot compel you to give it your loyalty and support in the unthinking manner that it has come to expect. As I mentioned at the outset of this book, a possible solution to the dilemmas presented by the sports-industrial complex is to simply give up sports or, at the very least, to give up a specific team, league, or sport that causes you too much angst to continue to follow. But how do you proceed if you are unable to simply ignore the problematic aspects of sports but you still want to remain a fan?

PART II

HOW TO BE A FAN IN THE TWENTY-FIRST CENTURY

8
BE A FAIR-WEATHER FAN

I'm about to say something that is going to shock almost every sports fan out there. It's OK to be a fair-weather fan. It's OK to stop rooting for a team because they piss you off or because they stand for things you don't stand for. It's even OK to stop rooting for them because they lose too much, and it's OK to start rooting for another team because they win more. Or, for that matter, to swap out your fan allegiances for any number of other reasons or no real reason at all.

The idea flies in the face of just about everything every sports fan has been taught their entire lives. We're taught that at the heart of fandom lies loyalty and that the definition of loyalty involves sticking with whatever or whomever one is loyal to through thick and thin. Generally, that's a good policy in life, but why should it apply to sports? What has a professional sports team done for you to earn such loyalty? Where is it written that the team whose fandom you adopted when you were a kid—or the fandom you were likely born into—must stay the same forever? Nowhere I can find. Which makes sense. After all, are you still eating all the same foods, going to the same church, and voting for the same political party your parents did? Are you listening to the same music now that you listened to when you were twelve? Of course not. Our tastes and our views on all manner of things evolve as we grow up and get on with life, so why not our sports affiliations as well? Can we not change them as we see fit?

I believe we can. Indeed, I believe we should. In fact, in practice, I've switched my sports allegiances a number of times.

I did not grow up in a large multigenerational family, and the family I did have was not all that interested in sports. My parents, born and raised in Detroit, knew who the Tigers, Lions, Red Wings, and Pistons were and could, perhaps, name a few of the more famous members of those clubs, but they didn't play sports themselves, go to games, or pay all that much attention to the teams' fortunes. I was born and grew up in Flint, Michigan. I lived there for the first eleven years of my life, so when I independently began to take an interest in sports, that same sort of Detroit-by-osmosis fandom took hold as well.

Seeing my interest in sports, my parents took me to many Detroit Tigers games and to the odd football game, and they indulged my baseball card and memorabilia collecting and my modest personal athletic ambitions. But for the most part, my journey into fandom was a function of my own, solitary efforts that were dictated primarily by what I could watch on TV or listen to on the radio. Which is to say that I was never indoctrinated into fandom in the way so many people are. I was never told by an older sibling, parents, grandparents, or any uncles that the Detroit Tigers were inherently superior to other baseball teams or that in rooting for the Detroit Lions lay virtue. I liked to see those teams do well and was bummed when they did poorly, but the idea of having loyalty to them in any real sense wasn't part of the equation.

In early 1985, my family moved from Flint to West Virginia. Given the NFL's robust national TV package, I could still keep general tabs on the Lions from my new home. And given the ascent of the Pistons to the elite of the NBA in the mid-to-late 1980s, I was able to more or less maintain my basketball fix. But the Tigers were another matter. There was exactly one major network baseball game a week on TV back in those days, and though the Tigers were the defending World Series champions, the odds of them appearing on my TV any given Saturday were low. In those pre-internet days, you could not simply continue to watch your favorite teams via some league-owned streaming package, so watching the George Kell and Al Kaline-called games on WDIV was right out. The radio signal from WJR in Detroit, while mighty, was not mighty enough to consistently send Ernie Harwell's voice to my home among the hills, so my favorite way to consume Tigers games before I moved—on the radio—was gone as well. Baseball was my first love, and I had a near-daily need for it. I had to find another option.

Thanks to Superstation WTBS, I had that option: Atlanta Braves baseball, broadcast as a prestige-builder and as an accounting trick by Ted Turner, the owner of the network and the team, who made his real money with outdoor billboards, syndicated sitcoms, professional wrestling, and cable news. Thanks to him, even a kid in West Virginia—or Oklahoma or Oregon—could see Major League Baseball games almost every day. Even if I would still say, for a couple of years at least, that the Detroit Tigers were my favorite team, if someone had asked me, my habit of watching 140+ Braves games a year turned me into a Braves fan in fairly short order. It was not because they were good. Indeed, the mid-1980s Atlanta

Braves were arguably the worst team in baseball. It was not because they presented a greater example of virtue or admirability than the Tigers, if even such a thing could be measured. It was because, quite simply, they were there.

My family would return to Michigan to visit for many years after we moved, and when I would return, I would catch all kinds of flak from cousins, friends, and former classmates who accused me of abandoning the Tigers. As if my former status as a Tigers fan wasn't a function of the same thing that made me a Braves fan now: the ability to see or hear the team on a regular basis. To watch or listen to the team's games and to follow its progress. In West Virginia, my ability to do that was due to their presence on cable television. In Michigan, it was an accident of birth. If anything, the former is a more rational basis for watching and rooting for a team than the latter, is it not?

My change in baseball fandom was because I moved and, as anyone who went to college in Boston and now claims to be a "lifelong" Red Sox fan can attest, a change in geography is a pretty common reason for allegiance-switching. But I've switched for other, far less rational reasons.

As a kid, I and everyone around me rooted for the Michigan Wolverines in football and basketball. No one in my family went to college there. We just happened to live there, I liked those sports, and rooting for the Wolverines was simply what one did. As was the case with the Lions and Pistons, it was still pretty easy to root for Michigan after I moved because their games were still on TV all the time in West Virginia, so there wasn't a big reason to shop my fandom around. In the fall of 1990, however, I applied to Michigan as an undergraduate, and they rejected me. They were right to do so, I will quickly admit, given my lackluster grades and SAT scores. Ohio State accepted me, though. I went to college there and subsequently switched my sports loyalties. I'd like to say that it was because I spent a fall on campus in Columbus and got swept up in school spirit, but that'd be a lie. I switched before I even moved into the dorms. I switched out of pure spite. I haven't regretted it. My daughter is now a senior in high school and has applied to Michigan, so I suppose we'll see if my grudges last longer than thirty years.

You can change who you root for even if you've never left your hometown and even if you didn't attend their rival. You can decide to root for another team for any reason or for no reason at all. Indeed, you can switch which team you root for simply because they suck.

That's the one that will cause sports fans to howl the most loudly. After all, isn't victory all the sweeter when you've endured defeat? If you abandon a team when they're at a low, do you not lose out on that ecstatic, once-in-a-lifetime feeling when they finally hoist that championship trophy? Don't you forgo the opportunity to reminisce with fellow fans about what it was like to root for the team when it was at its lowest once they finally reach the highest of heights? To revel in shared tradition, shared history, shared suffering, shared misery, and then, finally, at long last, shared celebration? Maybe. But such a thing is pretty overrated.

It's overrated because the happiness that comes from victory is fleeting. It may even be a delusion. Psychologists refer to a phenomenon called durability bias, which is one's belief that an event-driven feeling of happiness will bring lasting happiness. But such things rarely do. This even goes for big, personal, momentous things like getting a promotion and getting married, so it goes without saying that it applies to a sports team you support when they win a championship too.

Perhaps the best example of this can be seen with the multimedia sports personality Bill Simmons, who rose to fame lamenting his lot as a long-suffering Boston sports fan. When, in 2004, the Red Sox finally won their first World Series in eighty-six years, Simmons wrote a book about the experience entitled *Now I Can Die in Peace*.

Around the same time, when the New England Patriots were just beginning a near twenty-year run of dominance that saw them win six Super Bowls, Simmons wrote a still-cited column for ESPN in which he set forth the so-called "Rules for Being a True Fan," one of which was the so-called "five-year rule," which Simmons defined like this:

> After your team wins a championship, they immediately get a five-year grace period: You can't complain about anything that happens with your team (trades, draft picks, salary-cap cuts, coaching moves) for five years. There are no exceptions. For instance, the Pats could finish 0-80 over the next five years and I wouldn't say a peep. That's just the way it is. You win the Super Bowl, you go on cruise control for five years. Everything else is gravy.

Anyone even remotely familiar with Simmons's work knows that the Red Sox winning the World Series—they've actually won four since 2004—did not bestow peace upon his sports fan sensibilities. Nor did he, at any time, go five years without complaining about them, the Patriots, or the Boston Celtics after any of them won titles. He continues to complain and nitpick whatever moves the

Boston teams make and continues to be made miserable by their losses and failures, big and small. Their triumphs, meanwhile, stick with him for an even shorter time now than they did eighteen years ago. It's not because he's a hypocrite. It's because he was simply wrong about the level of satisfaction rooting for a championship team can bring. It's great in the moment, sure, but that feeling won't last.

At least with Boston sports fandom, there has been far more good than bad over the past few decades, so the idea of simply giving them up because they're bad isn't all that reasonable. What do you do, though, if the team whose fandom you inherited is terrible for years? What if, for any small glimmer of competitiveness they might show, they dwell in the cellar for a decade? Or for two?

Say you're a thirty-five-year-old basketball fan from Minneapolis, and as a child, when you were first drawn to the sport, you began rooting for the Minnesota Timberwolves. The Timberwolves franchise began play in the 1989–90 season, when you were a toddler. When you were ten years old, they posted their first winning season ever, powered by their young star Kevin Garnett. Over the next six years, the Timberwolves made the playoffs every year. They bowed out of the playoffs in the first round in all but one of those years, but it was still a pretty good time to be a Timberwolves fan. But then, starting in 2004–05, when you were seventeen, they went on a run where they missed the playoffs sixteen out of seventeen years and counting. And when they missed, they missed big, finishing in last or second-to-last in their division in all but one of those years. Even in the one year they made the playoffs in that run, they backed in as a fourth place finisher in a five-team division.

In late February 2021, the Timberwolves lost a game to the Phoenix Suns, and in doing so, they achieved a dubious distinction: they became the worst team in the history of professional sports, as measured by winning percentage. Not just basketball; *all* of professional sports. With their .39307 winning percentage over thirty-two seasons, they dipped below the NFL's Tampa Bay Buccaneer's .39321 winning percentage over forty-six seasons. If you're that thirty-five-year-old Timberwolves fan, they did that by being absolutely dreadful for over half of your life. Is that sort of long-standing terrible performance worth your unconditional devotion? Will a theoretical championship in, say, 2025 or 2030 be worth decades of misery? And what if it *never* comes?

I'd argue that it wouldn't be worth it. Indeed, I'd argue that such unconditional devotion even begins to contribute to the team's futility at some point, giving the Timberwolves' incompetent management license to continue to demonstrate further incompetence. Or to continue tanking if that's what they're doing. As long as you're still buying tickets, watching them on TV, and purchasing the team's merchandise, you're enabling it. Enabling it in a way that can be quantified. When the billionaire Glen A. Taylor bought the Timberwolves in 1994, he paid around $90 million for them. In 2021, he sold the team for over a billion dollars. More than a thousand percent premium, thanks in large part to the unconditional devotion of a heck of a lot of basketball fans who probably would've been happier if they had switched to the Milwaukee Bucks or the Indiana Pacers a decade ago.

I'm not saying that a bad year or three should cause you to start looking around for someone else to root for, but at some point, that kind of consistent losing—the sort of losing the Timberwolves, or the Pittsburgh Pirates, or the Detroit Lions, or the Buffalo Sabres have been up to for so long—gives a fan license to switch loyalties. Watching sports is supposed to be fun, and there's nothing fun about losing year after year after year. No one is going to give you a loyalty trophy for your suffering.

Another reason to switch teams you root for is because its owners and management are loathsome. To be sure, this is a relative thing. It has been said that every billionaire is a policy failure. It could be added that anyone rich enough and powerful enough to be able to purchase a professional sports team in this new Gilded Age is going to carry with them a great deal of baggage. Some, though, carry more baggage than others.

Some are *more* adept at bilking taxpayers and municipalities for handouts, and some are *more* transparent about subordinating their team's winning to their own personal enrichment. While the great majority of sports owners and executives are conservatives, some—like the Ricketts family, which owns the Chicago Cubs; the DeVos family, which owns the Orlando Magic; and Ken Kendrick of the Arizona Diamondbacks—have deep ties to Trumpist politics and are donors to or are even active in some of the nastiest political campaigns. Daniel Snyder of the Washington football team spent years and years trying do everything he could to keep that team's racist former name, all while presiding over a front office in which sexism and sexual harassment was ignored and, in some cases, encouraged. James Dolan of the New York Knicks was charged by the National Labor Relations Board with illegally threatening to withhold employee pay unless the employees voted against joining a union. Marge Schott, the one-time owner of the Cincinnati Reds, and Donald Sterling, the one-time owner of the Los Angeles Clippers, were both forced to sell their clubs after each made the vilest racist statements imaginable, with Schott going so far as to praise Adolf Hitler. These are just a few examples. A full accounting of the transgressions against ethics, morals, laws, and taste on the part of professional sports owners could fill numerous volumes.

I'm not suggesting that fans refuse to root for *any* team whose ownership or executive class offends their sensibilities because, again, these guys are billionaires, and given how billionaires roll, if one were to adopt that standard, one would quickly run out of teams to root for. Even if one attempted to organize their fandom in such a fashion, it would be pretty exhausting to keep ethical tabs on every owner and every executive for every team for which you might consider rooting. I generally know which sports figures are in legal trouble or which have said questionable things or have taken questionable ethical positions at any given time, but that's because I write about this stuff for a living. Expecting most sports fans to know all of that is a bit much. Say what you want about the tenets of rooting for laundry, but at least it's a more easily assumable ethos.

But at some point, a team's ownership or its executives can step in it so squarely and so publicly that it's difficult to ignore. At that point, it's totally legitimate to say that you no longer wish to support that team and find one with a less-objectionable billionaire in charge.

———————

A final reason to change rooting interests? Because you just simply *want* to. Because on some gut, emotional level, it just makes sense.

Despite the fact that I have been a baseball writer for most of my children's lives, I've never pushed sports on them. Far from it, actually. I took them to some minor league baseball games when they were very young, and they would, from time to time, watch baseball games on TV with me, but it was all very low-key, and they didn't otherwise take that much of an interest. Around the time they turned seven and eight, however, my son and daughter entered a brief period of heightened baseball fandom. During that period, they decided that they liked the Los Angeles Dodgers. That was sort of confusing. After all, I was a Braves fan, so I hadn't foisted the Dodgers on them in any serious way. They likewise weren't staying up until midnight watching baseball games from the West Coast. It was all sort of accidental and, in many ways, superficial.

In 2012, we took a family vacation to California, and they decided that California was some sort of paradise and that Los Angeles was glamorous because that's where TV and the movies came from. So if they were going to like a baseball team, it's not shocking that it'd be a California baseball team.

Adding to this was the fact that the Dodgers were in the news a lot around then because of their outfielder Yasiel Puig's sensational exploits and the controversies that surrounded him, which were the subject of conversations on podcasts and radio segments I recorded in the house and which they overheard. When, after one of those radio segments, my son asked me who Yasiel Puig was, it led me to explain to him the idea of both (a) Cuban players risking their lives to come to this country to play baseball; and (b) iconoclastic players who enrage stodgy old men and institutions. Both of those ideas appealed to him greatly. Around that same time, I was watching a Dodgers game one afternoon when my daughter asked me who was pitching. I told her it was Clayton Kershaw. Eventually, that led to me explaining to her that Clayton Kershaw was the best pitcher in baseball, which he was then. At that time, my daughter was someone who took great interest in the concept of people being "the best" at something, and thus Clayton Kershaw appealed to *her* greatly.

My kids' Dodgers fandom, or interest in baseball for that matter, never became particularly deep or serious. Both of the kids asked me to get them Dodgers shirts and merchandise when I was at the Dodgers' spring training camp in Arizona one year. My son put up a pennant on his bedroom wall. They asked me to take them to Cincinnati to see a game when the Dodgers visited the Reds, and so we went. A few years ago, I took them back to California, and we went to a game at Dodger Stadium, but by then, their interest in baseball was waning. They got new Dodgers gear that trip, but at that point, it was more about fashion statements and advertising their trip to California to their friends. Apart from Clayton Kershaw, I doubt either of them could name a single member of the team now, and apart from a couple of in-person games like that, I don't think either of them has watched baseball in a few years now. Sports are just not a part of their lives.

But a funny thing happened during their brief

period of Dodgers fandom, such as it was. When they got Dodgers shirts and merchandise, I bought some for myself so I could wear what they wore for that trip to Cincinnati, that trip to Los Angeles, or for the odd games that might've been on TV. As all this of this was happening, the Braves were in a competitively fallow period and the Dodgers were winning a lot, so I had greater cause to watch Dodgers games for professional reasons. Later, as my kids' interest in baseball fell off and they began to lead more independent, teenaged lives, those memories of that brief period when they at least superficially shared an interest of mine became more important to me. My memories of that connection are inextricably intertwined with Dodgers baseball.

Aligning oneself with any particular team is almost always an arbitrary act. It might be dictated by geography, such as when I became a Tigers fan because I happened to be born in Michigan, which is, by definition, mere accident of birth. It might be because of media exposure, such as when I became a Braves fan because I was able to see them on Superstation TBS, which was a function of a billboard mogul's belief that he could turn a UHF TV station into a powerhouse via cheap content like *I Love Lucy* reruns and Major League Baseball games. It might be because you have some emotional tie to a team that has far less to do with the team itself than with some tangential memories associated with it, like me, my kids, and the Dodgers—who, here, for the first time, I am finally admitting that I like more than the Braves and who I now consider to be my baseball team.

The Dodgers have brought me joy in recent years. The Braves, in large part because of the team's culture, its insistence on using native iconography, and the way in which it has continued to fleece taxpayers and turn its back on its Black fans in Atlanta, have caused me agita. Yes, I watched them win the World Series in 2021. And yes, I got some degree of enjoyment out of that, but I enjoyed them much more back in the 1980s when they lost a lot. So why should I stick with them now? What have they done for me?

9
ROOT FOR THE PLAYERS

If abandoning the laundry you've rooted for your whole life for some new team is a line you just can't cross, consider it a baby step. Root for players, not teams.

In my case, saying I'm no longer a Braves fan doesn't cause me a lot of stress, even if it's a way in which I've identified myself for decades, because there is absolutely nothing stopping me from enjoying watching their star right fielder Ronald Acuña Jr. or their MVP first baseman Freddie Freeman play. I don't have to stop watching them because I don't identify as a Braves fan first and foremost anymore. I still get to see them hit massive homers and run down balls in the gap as often as I want. No one can stop me. Is this not how so many people, somehow, became Chicago Bulls fans in the 1990s? Weren't the Bulls simply a Michael Jordan and Scottie Pippen delivery system? Once their era was over, tons of people moved on to other rooting interests, and while a lot of ink was spilled about the illegitimacy of being a fair-weather fan, that ink never resulted in a convincing argument.

Above all else, though, I know from experience that rooting for players, as opposed to teams, is meaningful. Indeed, rooting for a particular player, as opposed to a team, provided me with the most meaningful experience I've ever had while watching sports.

Around the time my Braves fandom was waxing in the 1980s, the Chicago Cubs called up a young pitcher named Greg Maddux. Maddux intrigued me to some extent because he was pretty good pretty early, but since I was a Braves fan, I didn't pay him much mind. Eventually, however, Maddux joined the Braves via free agency, and I watched nearly every one of his starts. Maddux, who by then had developed into the best pitcher in all of baseball, soon became my favorite player. I pored over all of his mind-boggling statistics and dreamed about the action on his two-seam fastball. His starts were appointment viewing for me for a decade because he was the Braves' ace. At least I thought that's why I watched Greg Maddux.

When Maddux had signed with Atlanta, I was a nineteen-year-old college student. Now flash forward to 2006 when I was a thirty-three-year-old married lawyer with two kids. Maddux had left the Braves to rejoin the

Chicago Cubs two years before. Though not objectively old yet, I felt old. I felt like the world was beating me and that whenever one could say I had been at my best, that time had long since passed. I got joy from time with my children and joy from escaping into baseball, but otherwise, my job and various sources of stress in my life had me feeling completely cooked.

One day that August, my law firm comped a bunch of us tickets to a Dodgers-Reds game down in Cincinnati. Maddux, certainly past his pitching prime by that point, had just been traded to the Dodgers from the Cubs and was pitching for Los Angeles that evening. He was something of a mercenary by then, a hired gun whom his employers hoped still had enough muscle memory left from his 1990s prime to help them out. I was pleased to see that Maddux was going to pitch that night, but I was worried all the same. Like me, Maddux's best years were in the rearview mirror. In many ways, he was cooked just like I was. I wondered sometimes if he, like me, wondered where it all went and if he'd ever feel vital again. I wondered if watching him pitch at age forty would be difficult—both for what it said about him and what it said about me.

The game began. Maddux walked a guy early. Since control was always his calling card, the walk made me worry that it'd be a long night. He soon settled down, though, and started throwing bullets. One inning. Two innings. Three. Wait, five innings and the Reds hadn't scratched out a run. Wait a minute—they didn't even have a hit.

Maddux was throwing a no-hitter.

The sixth inning started. There was a long fly ball and . . . it was caught! Another . . . but caught! The third batter of the inning came up, and Maddux mowed him down. It was like it was 1995 all over again. Heck, it was better than 1995. Even in his prime, Maddux never threw a no-hitter. His control was too good and he was around the plate too much. He couldn't *not* throw strikes. It just seemed to bother him. That's why he always, eventually, gave up hits. Here he was now, though, unhittable in his twenty-first year in the big leagues, in a three-quarters-empty park on a sleepy, steamy Thursday evening where there was hardly anyone rooting for him. But as he walked off the mound at the end of six, I was cheering at the top of my lungs, virtually alone.

The steamy night soon turned into a stormy night. As the top of the seventh began, the skies opened up and a deluge fell on Great American Ballpark. Lightning. Thunder. The Dodgers batted and the half-inning ended just as the umpires called for the tarp. For forty minutes, we stood under the overhang in front of the concourse, trying to keep dry. I knew that there was no chance that Maddux was going to come out for the bottom of the seventh. He was forty. His arm would be tight after the rain delay. His ticket to the Hall of Fame was assured already. He didn't need the no-hitter for his legacy or his happiness. The Dodgers had picked him up for the stretch run, and they needed to save his arm. No one is what they once were, and there was no reason whatsoever to push him.

The game resumed in the bottom of the seventh with a twenty-nine-year-old reliever named Joe Beimel on the mound. He gave up a hit to the first batter he faced, ending the would-be no-hitter. The Dodgers would hang on, though, and ended up winning 3–0. Greg Maddux got the win. I got to see him pitch like he was in his prime again, and I got to see him leave the game before anyone remembered that he didn't have it anymore.

I was too old to have baseball heroes when Greg Maddux joined the Braves, and I never considered him a hero in the eleven years he pitched for them. But on August 3, 2006, Greg Maddux was heroic in my eyes. Not because he was once a Braves pitcher. Not because I knew nothing about him and could thus project all manner of heroism onto him. Rather, he was heroic because I knew everything.

I knew what it meant to feel old and past my prime. I knew what it felt like to remember when I could do anything but not be able to will myself to do it like I once had. That night, Greg Maddux reminded me that even when you're not the best anymore, you can still do your best. That if you try your hardest and if things break right for you, you can still emerge victorious and, possibly, even triumphant though your best days are behind you. Maddux reminded me that in many ways, it's even *more* satisfying to triumph under such circumstances than it is to triumph when everyone expects you to. As I write this, that game was fifteen years ago. As I sit here now, I no longer believe that my best days are behind me. Somehow, I stopped believing that on August 3, 2006. Greg Maddux taught me otherwise. That night he, a single player, taught me more and meant more to me than any team ever had.

For a while after that game, I wondered what rooting for Greg Maddux, Los Angeles Dodger, meant for my relationship with the Atlanta Braves. Should I be mad that they had let him walk away a few years before? Should I feel guilty that I wanted to see another team— an occasional rival of the Braves at that—do well with a former Braves player? After tossing it around a bit, I asked myself: Why in the hell should I have any greater loyalty to a team than I have to a player who, as a human being, is far more relatable to me than a piece of intellectual property controlled by the sports-industrial complex? By the same token, I soon came around to the notion that if a player I rooted for by simple virtue of the team which employed him turned out to be a jackass of some kind, why should I be in any way obligated to continue to wish him well? Or to wish the team he played for success in spite of him being a jackass? Why, like so many do when someone on the team they support steps in it or acts maliciously, should I defend him?

There's nothing inherent in one's enjoyment of sports that requires an unwavering commitment to a single player or team over the course of one's lifetime. You can change your allegiances on a dime if you want to. You can decide, the moment the playoffs begin, that you love Kawhi Leonard and are going to be a Clippers fan for the next six weeks, even if you normally root for the Rockets. You can root for certain players on one team and certain players on a rival. What difference does it make? There aren't any rules here. You can be a fan of whoever—or whatever—you want.

10
BE A CASUAL FAN

In early November of 2017, my wife and I wanted to go to one of our favorite restaurants where we live in Columbus, Ohio. The problem: the restaurant is a really popular one, it was 6:30 p.m. on a Saturday, and we hadn't planned ahead and made a reservation. Normally we'd just do something else, but we were really craving the place so we decided to go anyway and try to maybe muscle our way into a couple of seats at the bar. If we had to wait, well, we'd wait. When we got to the restaurant a little after 7:00, however, it was half-empty and there were plenty of tables to choose from. Confused, we asked the host up front why the place wasn't jam-packed like it normally would have been.

"The Buckeyes are losing," she said. "We get a lot of cancellations when that happens. Especially when it's bad like this."

I looked up to the TV above the bar and, yep, OSU, which had been ranked number three in the nation, was down 48–17 midway through the fourth quarter to a not particularly good Iowa team. That loss would, eventually, keep Ohio State out of that year's four-team national championship playoff. I didn't even realize the Buckeyes were playing. Which, if you had known me even a few years before that, would've shocked you.

I entered Ohio State as a freshman in the fall of 1991. Despite what a lot of people think, Ohio State is a big school, and it's actually pretty easy to avoid football altogether if one wishes to, but I wasn't one of those people and didn't *want* to be one of those people. I, almost immediately, became a huge Buckeyes fan. I got student tickets, went to tailgates and games, and went to drunken watch parties when the team played on the road. I kept that fandom up all four years I was at OSU, stuck with them when I moved away for law school for three years, and threw myself back into it even more intensely when I moved back to Columbus in 1998. In all, I'd remain deeply immersed in Ohio State football and Ohio State football culture for around twenty years. It's easy to do when you live in Columbus. Indeed, it's harder to *not* be an Ohio State fan in Columbus in some ways than it is to be one.

Even if you haven't lived in a place like Columbus, you have known a hardcore fan of one team or another.

Maybe you've even been one. Someone who lives or dies with each game and each season. Someone who has owned the gear. Someone who has an encyclopedic knowledge of team history. Someone who not only knows the rivalries but knows how and why they started and can rattle off the flash points from those rivalries, like that beanball from the opposing pitcher in 2013 or that disrespectful quote from the other team's head coach in 2004. Maybe you're someone who owns novelty T-shirts that celebrate some transitory moment that briefly went viral a decade ago, and maybe you're someone who gets special joy when another fan nods at it in recognition. Maybe you're someone who not only knows every player on the active roster but knows the backups on the taxi squad and who the team's general manager is eyeing for the first few rounds of next year's draft or, at the very least, should be.

It's easy to criticize such fans. And it's easy to parody them. They are, in many respects, the personification of excess and obsession that, in almost any other pursuit, we would consider to be unhealthy. I don't actually *know* if that's unhealthy or, if it *is* unhealthy, *how* unhealthy it is. I'll leave that to the psychologists. But due to my nearly thirty years of living in Columbus, I do at least understand it. I've experienced what it feels like to be among like-minded people and what it feels like for a whole city to seemingly come together after a big win. It can be intoxicating. But I've also experienced how miserable the whole damn city can be when the Buckeyes lose. How it can cast a pall over the rest of the weekend. Make people grumpy. Beyond grumpy, even. The city and most of the state of Ohio lives for Buckeyes football, but it also dies with it sometimes, and it can be a real drag.

On January 6, 2009, it was a drag. The Buckeyes had lost to Texas in the Fiesta Bowl the night before. Texas was favored, so it was not like it was an upset loss or anything, but people were still miserable. I was pretty miserable too. It was Ohio State's third straight bowl loss. As early as the next morning, it was being reported that a number of star underclassmen were going to leave and declare early for the NFL draft. Between all of that and the fact that it was going to be months and months before another game, my mood was pretty dour.

Late that afternoon, I was playing with my three year-old son and found myself still distracted by college football stuff. For whatever reason, I realized that day, in ways that I had not realized it before, that my obsession with Buckeyes football was unhealthy for me. That it was consuming too much of my time and my emotional energy and interfering with other far more important parts of my life. I didn't make any grand declarations to myself or to anyone else, but I decided that afternoon that it'd be better for me if I backed away a bit and got a little more balance when it came to college football. I had no plans to *cease* being a fan, but I did decide to limit Ohio State football intake to the games themselves. I attempted to view them as defined, three-hour TV shows that I watched for the purpose of entertainment, to cut out most of the hype and things that surrounded them, and to do what I could to put the games out of my mind once they were over. In short, I decided to become a casual fan.

It was a lot easier to do that in January, when there wasn't much in the way of college football news and hype, than it might've been in September, so I was able to start small. I deleted the bookmarks to most of the OSU-related websites I visited. I stopped reading the local paper's breathless, daily, wall-to-wall coverage that is a year-round thing in Columbus. When OSU spring practice began, which gets more hype than the regular season of some college programs, I immersed myself in baseball, which I had begun writing about professionally on a part-time basis that April. When training camp began late that summer and the countdown to the regular season began,

I made a point to not watch the midweek and pregame Buckeyes-related TV shows like I always had in the past. At best, I read a couple of preseason preview articles about the team, sticking to the more superficial ones in national media as opposed to the intense, insider-friendly coverage of OSU-specific media outlets. I went into the first game of the season as the closest thing I had been to a casual college football fan in nearly twenty years.

And it was kind of great. I was still conversant enough with the team, thanks to holdover knowledge and from watching on Saturdays, to allow me to retain the Ohio State football literacy expected of a resident of Columbus, Ohio. I was still able to appreciate the cultural benefits that sports fandom brings, such as having natural and easy icebreakers in conversations with coworkers and the like. And of course, I still watched the games and enjoyed the games for what they were. At the same time, my lack of an obligation to keep tabs on anything and everything was a massive time-saver, and not putting myself in positions where I was reliving the last game and being anxious about the next game provided considerable emotional relief. The Buckeyes lost the second game of the season that year to USC, at home no less, and looked pretty bad in the process. Old posts that pop up in my Facebook memories each fall remind me that I was pretty cranky about the game as it was happening, but before I went to sleep that night, I just shook it off and let it go in ways I never would've before. That continued all through the fall. I had cheered through better Ohio State seasons—national championship Ohio State seasons even—but never had I felt more content with an Ohio State season as I did that year. I even attended a game in person at Ohio Stadium that fall and enjoyed it immensely, precisely because I approached it as a casual fan.

There was another benefit of casual fandom. It gave me a new perspective on a thing that happens within passionate fandoms of all stripes: gatekeeping.

I was about a year into my casual OSU fandom when I backslid a bit. Just before the 2010 season began, I logged onto an old Ohio State message board I used to frequent. There was a good deal of turnover on the team, and having completely avoided news about recruiting, spring practice, and the position battles in summer camp, I wasn't super familiar with all the players who'd be important to the team in the upcoming season. To try to catch up a little bit, I clicked on a couple of discussion threads where people were talking about all of that. Once there, I came across some other fans who were asking some pretty basic questions, the sorts of which I'd have known off the top of my head two years earlier but which I did not know the answer to now. When scrolling through the answers, I was shocked at the hostility of some of the respondents, many of whom shamed the person who had asked the question in the first place and mocked them for their ignorance. I was familiar with that sort of "oh, you like Pavement, name three of their albums" fan snobbery that existed in music, comics, and various other fan cultures, but before then, I hadn't considered how prevalent it was in the world of hard-core sports fandom. Probably because, not too long before, I had never been a target of it in sports.

I felt attacked by that gatekeeping in certain ways, but I also felt ashamed, because I realized that a year or two previously, I may have very well taken on the same attitude as the gatekeepers in those threads. It took being on the outside, even just a little bit, for me to appreciate how toxic that sort of thing can be. In the years since, especially after I began working in sports media professionally, I have become sensitive to it elsewhere. Especially in baseball, which I still follow fairly obsessively, I have noted just how prominent a weapon such gatekeeping is for men who seek to exclude women from a given fandom. Since then, I've tried hard not to be that person when talking about sports with someone who may not be as knowledgeable as I am. When I encounter a casual fan who doesn't know a cool thing about baseball that I know, I view it as an opportunity to tell a great story to a new audience, and that's a pretty wonderful feeling.

That sort of ugliness notwithstanding, being a casual fan of Ohio State football for a couple of years allowed me to learn new things about the team and the sport with something at least approaching a joy and satisfaction one experiences with the truly novel. Seeing a player in a game situation for the first time and not knowing what he might do was cool in a way it never would've been if I had watched a bunch of uploaded videos of him from his high school days or if I had possessed a set of expectations for him that must be met lest I be disappointed. It was a fandom of observation of the new and the entertaining as opposed to a fandom of obligation one possesses when one is committed to following something intensely. I became a fan that was less driven by tribalism, community, and negatively reinforced emotion and one who began to appreciate the aesthetics of the sport and the beauty the sport often displayed. I was also able to find enjoyment in the game despite occasional losses and setbacks, and those losses and setbacks no longer consumed me or affected my moods or self-esteem. It just seemed way healthier.

But it also did something else: it led to the *end* of my being a college football fan.

———————

Casual fandom brings with it a certain perspective-changing distance. It brings with it a certain objectivity that intense fans who live and breathe a sport tend to lack. It causes you to drop the "we" when talking about the teams you root for and causes you to spend less time behaving as though you are part of the team. When you drop intense fandom, you lose that part of your identity that is necessarily intertwined with the teams or the sports you love, and you thus lose that impulse to reflexively defend them against criticism, which you may have previously perceived as an attack.

Which means that, over the course of 2009 and 2010, my reading a lot of stuff and watching a number of TV news features about the exploitation of amateur athletes and the ethical shortcomings and sometimes outright corruption of the NCAA and big-time college sports programs like Ohio State's hit different, as the kids say. Those articles and features didn't present information that was unknown to me just a few years prior, when I lived and breathed Ohio State football. I had just excised from my brain that part of me which previously would've had defenses and excuses at the ready because, on some primal level, I felt that hearing negative information about something that I loved was directed at me as well. Through my casual fandom, I allowed myself to be receptive to criticisms of college sports and the Ohio State football program in ways that I never would've allowed myself to be before. I allowed myself to appreciate, in ways that I should've appreciated long before, just how badly college football players are exploited by the NCAA and universities which make millions—collectively billions—on the back of athletes' unpaid labor. I allowed myself to appreciate the wringer through which college football players' bodies are put and how it is no less destructive to them than the NFL wringer is to professional players, even if it's not as noticeable due to their youth and seeming resilience.

Being objective and receptive to such things does not require one to turn one's back on the sport or the team that one loves—I spend more time hurling criticism at Major League Baseball than just about anyone and my love of that game has not waned—but in the case of college sports, my casual fan objectivity eventually compelled me to give up watching college football altogether. It was not long after that year's Sugar Bowl between the Buckeyes and the

Arkansas Razorbacks—which I enjoyed a great deal—that I thought to myself that I couldn't stick with the sport much longer given all that I know about it. I didn't make a hard and fast decision about it, but on September 3, 2011, the Buckeyes opened their season against Akron. For the first time that I could remember, I didn't turn the game on. And I haven't watched a college football game since.

As I've said elsewhere in this book, one need not give up their fandom entirely simply because one has ethical or moral issues with certain aspects of sports. My experience with college football was a personal decision that not everyone must make. But it's certainly the case that there is nothing in the fan rulebook that says one has to be fanatical about sports. There is nothing that requires one to be a hard-core sports fan who is aware of every player, every stat, and every detail about the teams one roots for. It takes a lot of time and energy to keep up with that stuff, and as I've noted already, the very thing to which one is devoting all of that time and energy is, often, kind of depressing or stands for things that are antithetical to one's values and interests. And, like me, it can make you a miserable stick in the mud sometimes.

It's totally acceptable to be a casual fan. Indeed, it may be easier to be a casual fan in sports than it is in anything else. If one is kinda sorta into Bob Dylan, one might find themselves really, really lost if they just pick up one of his weird late-1970s Christian albums and give it a spin. I have no idea how one can make any sort of sense out of a Marvel movie at this point if they haven't seen most of the ones that have come out over the past decade-plus.

In contrast, a lot of people who don't watch much soccer can tune into the World Cup and have fun. Every two years, the Olympics comes along and makes us all, suddenly and temporarily, fans of curling or gymnastics. Even if you're not super conversant or super invested, you should watch something if it brings you joy. You shouldn't put yourself in a position where your commitment and sense of obligation to something is so great that you watch it even if it *ceases* to bring you joy. Sports are supposed to be fun, right?

11
SUPPORT ACTIVISM

The irony of Colin Kaepernick's famous 2016 protests during the playing of the national anthem is that if it wasn't for the NFL's commitment to that conflation of patriotism and sports we discussed a couple of chapters ago, he would never have been in the position to take a knee in the first place. Indeed, he wouldn't have even been on the field.

For years, television considerations made it so that the national anthem would be played before the players left the locker room. The end of the song would cause the crowd to cheer wildly, and then, as they were cheering, the players would run out, bringing about a convergence of noise and spectacle that was perfect for the cameras. That little bit of hype would be enough, the TV and league executives figured, to keep fans in front of the TV long enough to see a couple of commercials just before kickoff. Then, in the years after 9/11 and the sports leagues' headlong dive into patriotism, paid-for and otherwise, the rules changed, and the NFL began telling teams that players needed to be on the sidelines for the anthem with their helmets under their arm as if they were something akin to soldiers themselves. Hardly anyone noticed the difference at the time, and hardly anyone noticed in 2016 when Kaepernick first sat down on a bench during the anthem before a preseason game and then, a couple of weeks later, began to take a knee.

Steve Wyche of NFL.com became the first reporter to ask Kaepernick about his protest. The San Francisco 49ers quarterback explained it thusly:

> I am not going to stand up to show pride in a flag for a country that oppresses Black people and people of color. To me, this is bigger than football and it would be selfish on my part to look the other way. There are bodies in the street and people getting paid leave and getting away with murder.

Kaepernick was, of course, referring to police killings of Black people and people of color. Kaepernick was soon joined by his teammate Eric Reid, who said that, "We chose to kneel because it's a respectful gesture. I remember thinking our posture was like a flag flown at half-mast to mark a tragedy." In November of that year, Lindsay Gibbs and Aysha Khan of *ThinkProgress* wrote an article entitled "Tracking the Kaepernick Effect: The Anthem Protests Are Spreading." They noted that by that point, forty-nine NFL players from thirteen teams had knelt, sat, or raised a fist during the national anthem before games and that three teams had linked arms or held hands as a sign of unity. And it was not limited to football:

> Fourteen WNBA players from three teams protested in the playoffs. Star soccer player Megan Rapinoe took a knee during the anthem during a NWSL game, and later when representing the U.S. national team. Gold medal swimmer Anthony Ervin raised a fist as the anthem played during a meet in Brazil. Eight NBA teams have joined arms in unity. Even national anthem singers are taking a knee. Perhaps most significantly, protests during the anthem have occurred in at least 52 high schools, 43 colleges, one middle school, and two youth leagues in 35 states across the country and three nations abroad.

To say the public was divided is an understatement. On the one hand, the protests were praised by many, and replicas of Kaepernick's jersey became the best-selling piece of merchandise in sports. President Obama said, "I think he cares about some real, legitimate issues that have to be talked about." On the other hand, a massive backlash ensued, beginning of all places within the NFL, where commissioner Roger Goodell told the Associated Press, "I don't necessarily agree with what he's doing . . . we believe very strongly in patriotism in the NFL. I personally believe very strongly in that." Drew Brees, the quarterback of the New Orleans Saints, told ESPN that Kaepernick "can speak out about a very important issue. But there's plenty of other ways that you can do that in a peaceful manner that doesn't involve being disrespectful to the American flag."

That idea—that Kaepernick was disrespecting the flag, or the military, or police officers, or the United States, as opposed to lodging a cogent protest—would take deep root among those who took issue with him and what he was doing. In the coming months and years, he would be vilified by President Donald Trump, which in turn made Kaepernick a popular punching bag for conservative media personalities and political candidates.

Fans would become deeply divided, with some claiming that the protests and other instances in which athletes voiced opinions on matters of social justice had turned them off of sports completely. The phrases "stick to sports" and "shut up and dribble"—first applied to LeBron James by conservative culture warrior Laura Ingraham—would become a mantra for those who wanted to pretend that sports and the athletes who compete in them were not a part of broader society.

Kaepernick would play out the 2016 season and would opt out of his contract in order to latch on with a team better than the 2–14 San Francisco 49ers, but no one signed him. The last game he ever played in the NFL came on January 1, 2017, a 25–23 loss to the Seattle Seahawks. He and Reid filed grievances against the NFL, alleging that they had been blackballed. Given the parade of quarterbacks far less talented than him who have gotten jobs in the ensuing years, Kaepernick undoubtedly *was* blackballed. The NFL eventually reached a seven-figure settlement with him to resolve the case.

Kaepernick's playing career was over, but he would remain an icon of social activism. First as a spokesman for Nike, which has long associated itself with social justice messaging, sometimes as a matter of fashion, sometimes more substantively. He'd go on to become far more influential as a model for later athlete protests and the larger Black Lives Matter movement following the murders of Ahmaud Arbery, Breonna Taylor, and George Floyd in 2020. That year, athletes and even some coaches across the major sports leagues began to speak out, echoing Kaepernick's words and his take-a-knee posture. Even the leagues would fall in line.

That falling into line was not uniform or seamless, of course. As protests broke out across the country in late May and early June of 2020, the NBA immediately issued a statement supporting them. Basketball courts featured Black Lives Matter decals, jerseys were printed with "Say Their Names" and similar messages on the back in place of players' names, and postgame interviews often dealt exclusively with social justice. After the August 23, 2020, shooting of Jacob Blake in Kenosha, Wisconsin, players boycotted games until the NBA agreed to open arenas as polling places for the upcoming election. The NFL, in contrast, was silent until over a dozen stars released a video demanding that the league speak out. Commissioner Goodell responded with his own video, saying he should have listened to players earlier. He also gave an interview in which he claimed that he wished he had handled the Kaepernick protests differently four years earlier. There would eventually be something of a coordinated messaging effort from the league on the Black Lives Matter movement, even if it was a belated one.

Major League Baseball resumed play in late July 2020 after the COVID-driven delay to the start of the season. On opening day, the league made a ceremonial gesture of having players and coaches kneel before—but not during— the national anthem while holding a large black ribbon as a display of unity. While not exactly a bold statement, for baseball, which is a far whiter and more conservative institution than the NBA and NFL, it was more than one might've expected. To be sure, the about-face from the leagues on athletes' social justice protests and messaging was something less than enthusiastic and genuine. Indeed, it was an exercise in co-option of the highest order, much like we've seen from corporations and institutions of all stripes in recent years. But still, half-hearted, superficial support is an improvement compared to the leagues' previous hostility.

There has been considerable discussion about fan reaction to athlete activism. Most of it is reduced to talk about polling or anecdotes of dubious value.

Polling in August 2020, when the post-George Floyd athlete protests were at their height with the start of the NFL season, found that more than seven of ten sports fans supported teams and athletes speaking out on issues of social justice and racial equality. Of the 71 percent of fans who supported athletes speaking out, 44 percent *strongly* supported it. Nearly half of the fans surveyed said they were more likely to support teams and athletes who spoke out than they were the year before, while 20 percent said they were less likely to. There was likewise a clear divide on *where* fans believe social issues should be addressed in sports. Fifty-one percent supported players expressing their views during sporting events, while 49 percent said they would prefer they do so off the court or field.

Of course, there was a strong political divide, with a far greater percentage of Republicans opposing social justice messaging from athletes. This was particularly clear when it came, specifically, to the national anthem as opposed to other modes of protest. There, 81 percent of self-identifying Republicans said that professional athletes should be required to stand for the anthem. Four years earlier, when Colin Kaepernick was just getting started, a similar poll on the same question resulted in 73 percent of self-identifying Republicans taking the position that pro athletes should stand for the anthem. For self-identifying Democrats, only 33 percent said pro athletes should be required to stand for the anthem in the 2020 poll. In 2016, 43 percent of self-identifying Democrats believed pro athletes should be required to stand. Overall, the number of respondents who believed pro athletes should be required to stand has dropped from 56 percent in 2016 to 54 percent in 2020.

Anecdotally, both sports and political media was littered with stories about fans who claimed that they stopped supporting their favorite team or stopped watching sports altogether because of an athlete's political statements. These stories, which seemed very much like those election year stories in which reporters behave as if the nation's political mood can be judged by who speaks to them in small-town diners, flew in the face of polling, which showed that moments of silence, social justice messages on jerseys, and even athletes engaging in political protests during sporting events were supported by a majority of fans surveyed. Such a sentiment was also not born out in any clear way in TV viewership or sports revenue numbers, though such numbers were way out of whack with historical trends due to the pandemic, the 2020 election, and the altered schedules for sports leagues that year.

How the public mood breaks down on this is interesting to me, but I'm struck by how often the conversation about that mood is cast in terms that basically assume that social justice activism on the part of athletes is something to be merely tolerated instead of embraced. As if it can only serve to push away fans and that the only material consideration at play is how far athletes can go down this road until a critical number of fans are repelled by it. You rarely hear about how, for some, seeing athletes and, in some cases, teams and leagues embrace social and racial justice can be a draw for fans. How it can serve to make sports more appealing as a vehicle for social change as opposed to mere entertainment. This, by the way, is an idea that is not aimed solely at those on the more conservative end of the political spectrum who believe that sports and social activism should remain separate. It's also aimed at those on the left who have historically underestimated or even discounted the role sports can play in the advancement of social justice.

That latter attitude goes back a century at least. Back to the early socialist idea that sports are nothing more than a tool of a capitalist ruling class. That the ideas and values communicated through sports serve, unconsciously or otherwise, as a means of indoctrinating people, especially young people, into a bourgeois ideology in which money, power, celebrity, corporatism, competition, and strict hierarchies are valued while workers—as embodied by the athletes themselves—are seen as disposable. Alongside that idea runs an idea that sports fandom, like religion, is an opiate of the masses. A tool of pacification of the labor force, which, without the distraction of a few games or matches each week—and the creation of a simulacrum of a meritocracy—might begin to appreciate that conditions in the real world are not, you know, fair and just.

There are some legitimate truths tied up in this dismissal of sports, but it's an unwise dismissal all the same. It's unwise because rejecting sports out of hand as an unsalvageable institution leaves us in the exact same place we'd be in if we rejected all social justice messages because they seem threatening to sports. With athletes' voices unheard. And with vast swaths of people, whose most significant exposure to ideas of social justice might be through sports, unreached.

The legendary sports columnist Lester Rodney was faced with this dilemma back in 1935. Rodney, a communist himself, disagreed with the notion set forth by the Communist Party of the United States that sports were an inherently bourgeois pursuit, destructive to the working class. He convinced the communist newspaper, the *Daily Worker*, to let him write a regular sports column as a means of counteracting that notion. In his first column, Rodney wrote this:

> It happens that baseball is the American national game. I would say that nine out of every ten American workers follow it intensely, as well as other sports. You can condemn them for it, if you are built that way, and you can call baseball a form of bourgeois opium for the masses. But that doesn't get around the fact that the vast ocean of Americans of whom we are yet a minority, adore baseball. Are we going to maintain our isolation and make Americans stop their baseball before we will condescend to explain Communism to them? When you run the news of a strike alongside the news of a baseball game, you are making American workers feel at home. It gives them the feeling that Communism is nothing strange or foreign. Let's loosen up. Let's prove that one can be a human being as well as a Communist.

Baseball is no longer as popular as it was when Rodney wrote that in 1935, and nearly ninety years later, one's need to explain "that one can be a human being as well as a Communist" may not be as pressing as it was for him. But the idea that sports and society exist side by side and that each can comment upon and inform the other remains relevant. Whether one comes at things from the left or the right, one should not be in the business of looking down one's nose at what athletes who are committed to social activism and social justice can accomplish, both substantively and in terms of spreading the message to people who need to hear it. To appreciate why this is, one need only look at the history of athlete activism.

Colin Kaepernick did not invent athlete protest in the face of social injustice. Indeed athletes—almost exclusively Black athletes—have long advocated for social and racial justice in the face of a conservative culture that would prefer that athletes—particularly Black athletes—remain silent. These movements came in at least three distinct waves, beginning with Joe Louis, Jesse Owens, and Jack Johnson providing symbolic victories during the Jim Crow era. A second wave of activist athletes rose after World War II, with Jackie Robinson, Kenny Washington, and Earl Lloyd breaking the color barriers in their respective sports and serving as a harbinger of the civil rights movement. A third wave of athlete activism took place alongside the Black Power movement with Muhammad Ali's rejection of the Vietnam War and John Carlos and Tommie Smith raising their fists on the podium at the 1968 Olympics.

These events and the figures who took part in them are widely praised today. Muhammad Ali was almost universally called a hero upon his death in 2016. Jackie Robinson has practically been canonized as a saint by Major League Baseball and its fans. Carlos and Smith are hailed for their bravery whenever their names and their protest are mentioned. At the time, however, they were largely scorned and vilified. Those moments are only venerated as historic moments now that they are safely in the past, and those athletes are only venerated as historic figures now that they are dead or, in the case of Carlos and Smith, decades past the point where they seem threatening to white America.

Sports fans can and should do more than merely tolerate athlete activism. We should actively root for it and actively support athletes engaged in it. We should root for it in the present, as it's happening, in ways that many now claim they would have if they had been around when Jackie Robinson first suited up for the Dodgers in 1947 or when Muhammad Ali was risking everything by refusing to be inducted into the army in 1967. We should root for it in ways in which those who came before us never did. We should try to think and act in solidarity with the athletes who bring us so much pleasure and entertainment. We should be keenly aware of the fact that some of the highest profile instances of political activism in recent years, from Colin Kaepernick to Megan Rapinoe, took place in stadiums—spaces that serve as the closest thing to public gathering spots outside of literal town squares and thus help shape and reflect the pressing issues of this historical moment—which have necessarily become sites of social and political struggle.

By doing so, we will be rooting for something greater than a mere sporting event. We will be rooting for the betterment of society.

12
EMBRACE METAFANDOM

In 1982, at ballparks all over the country, the Lipton Tea Company gave away posters with the covers of every World Series program on them. My brother and I got ours at Tiger Stadium in Detroit. From the day I brought mine home, the poster was always a fixture on my bedroom wall. The program covers were arranged in eight satisfying rows of nine and one row of six, with the 1903 program in the bottom right corner and the latest—1981—at the top left. Each program cover was clearly reproduced, with the type and photos legible. It was a colorful poster, highly pleasing to the eye. It invited long hours of study, and did I ever study it. Indeed, I studied it so much that nine-year-old me quickly memorized every World Series matchup in baseball history to that point.

But something else happened as a result of my intensive study: to this day, I am utterly incapable of thinking of any World Series that took place between 1903 and 1981 without instantly picturing the program cover. Even for those World Series of which I've subsequently seen highlights, or in some cases, entire games on video, it is the program cover that is emblazoned in my mind and in my memory, to the point where, to this day, it crowds out the actual events that transpired in those Fall Classics. The 1932 World Series is not about Babe Ruth's famous Called Shot, it's about the WPA-esque painting of a Yankees player sliding into home on the cover of the program. Mentioning the 1934 World Series does not, at least at first, bring to mind Dizzy Dean and the St. Louis Cardinals' famous Gashouse Gang; it makes me think of the large illustrated tiger, standing on its hind legs as it appeared on the poster and the program cover it depicted. The 1956 World Series doesn't conjure up images, like it does for so many, of Yogi Berra jumping into Don Larsen's arms after the latter had tossed the only perfect game in the history of the Fall Classic, it makes me think of managers Casey Stengel and Walter Alston pictured next to images of Yankee Stadium and Ebbets Field.

Which is weird, right? As I'm writing this, I've been a professional baseball writer for thirteen years. I've written plenty of decently researched articles about the World Series, and I've read scores of baseball books, almost all of which talk about the World Series at some point or another, and a least a dozen of which were specifically about the World

Series. There are a lot of people who know more about the history of the World Series than I do, but I'm pretty well versed. In light of that, is it not odd that this mere totem—a free giveaway poster from forty years ago—takes up more psychic space than everything I have since learned about World Series history? That these little thumbnail sketches of the program covers—many of which have little, if anything, to do with the actual matchups from a given year—continue to define the World Series for me?

I don't have a definitive answer, but I do have a word that I have tossed around for many years now and which I can't shake. The word is "metafan." The concept is that, in my case, at least as far as the World Series is concerned, my feelings about it are born of an abstraction based on that poster. A poster that first served to complete the idea of the World Series in my limited understanding that eventually consumed the idea, to the point where the real thing—the images, accounts, and descriptions of actual World Series games—have less room in which to flourish.

I'm not sure this is unique to me. I think almost all serious sports fans are, to some extent or another, metafans. People who came to sports—or at least came to love or obsess about sports—via something in addition to, or perhaps something completely other than, actually sitting down and watching them. There was a hook there, be it fantasy sports, video games, collecting memorabilia, reading or writing about sports, engaging in statistical analysis, or simply being friends with other sports fans that either drew them in deeper to sports fandom or took their fandom in other, less conventional directions. Or perhaps they're deeply into something that functions alongside sports but that is a step removed from them.

For example, I know a lot of people who intensely follow the hot stove season in baseball, during which free agents sign with new teams, trades are made, and considerable time is spent assessing the season that just passed and anticipating the one that is about to begin. Some of these people, however, think of the hot stove season as the real draw and find themselves in an odd place where they wonder if the tail isn't wagging the dog. When talking about the idea of metafandom for an article I wrote about the then-basic idea I had of it a decade ago, a friend emailed me this regarding the then-upcoming baseball season:

> There's a small part of me that's apprehensive about Opening Day. I spend so much time reading and writing about the game that I'm not sure when I'm actually going to find the time to watch it. The

scary thing is, for at least part of the offseason, that prospect doesn't really bother me. I kind of enjoy having the time away to decompress and actually keep up with the steady stream of baseball news. I'm often left wondering how long I could realistically maintain my all-consuming interest in baseball without actually, you know, watching a baseball game. Sometimes I almost have to remind myself that I have all these unread items to get to because I like baseball, and not the other way around.

There are forms of metafandom that are far more detached than even that. Even more attenuated from the actual playing of sports than just following its news. Forms that, in some cases, are detached from reality altogether.

People write sports fan fiction, for example, making up entire, alternate, and imagined reality stories about what goes on in real athletes' private lives and what happens in the professional lives of entirely made-up players. If people who write historical fiction or alt-history are called "history buffs," the people who read and write sports fanfic have to be considered sports fans, no?

A favorite book of mine, which is not fan fiction but rather something a couple of steps to the side of it, is Robert

Coover's 1968 novel, *The Universal Baseball Association, Inc., J. Henry Waugh, Prop.*, in which the protagonist plays out decades worth of seasons of his fictional, simulated baseball league with dice and a pencil, not unlike any number of fantasy or tabletop baseball games that would come into much greater fashion in later decades. In the book, Waugh's star pitcher, Damon Rutherford, is killed after being hit in the head with a comebacker following three consecutive rolls of triple snake eyes. It was an outcome mandated by a rule in the "Extraordinary Occurrences Chart," which Waugh himself wrote for a game he himself invented but which nonetheless throws him for an emotional loop because he is so invested. His commitment to his fake baseball league is so deep that he has imagined the players' personalities, their wives, their girlfriends, and even the bartenders at the bars where the players drink after games. Waugh is living in the game, not just as its creator but as a participant, his mirror neurons twitching and the portions of his brain devoted to empathy working overdrive. So of course, the death of one of his players hits him hard. Would Waugh, if he himself were real, be considered a baseball fan? I think he would have to be, even if his fandom is rooted in something completely removed from Major League Baseball as it functions in our particular plane of reality.

In 2020, an online game called *Blaseball* came out. The game, which is something of an absurdist simulation of baseball, pits fictional teams such as the Kansas City Breath Mints, the New York Millennials, and the Breckenridge Jazz Hands against one another in games featuring random events such as the incineration of players by rogue umpires, or a pitcher growing an extra finger. Like real baseball, games can be delayed by weather. Unlike real baseball, that weather could consist of peanuts falling from the sky. There's betting on outcomes. Fans can "idol" specific players and earn fake, in-game money based on their performance. Users are able to use their fake money to vote on events and rule changes every week. I've not played *Blaseball*, but I know some people who have, and despite its absurdity and disconnection from reality, they talk about it in ways that, while not exactly the kind of water cooler chatter you may have with a fellow fan the morning after a Dodgers-Giants game, are not *wholly* dissimilar to how traditional sports fans may discuss their rooting interests. At the very least, there's buy-in and connection that is every bit as real as actual sports fandom. And, of course, it appears to be a great deal of fun.

Even if one does not go quite as far out there to where they are writing novellas imagining a rich, fictitious inner life of NBA players, mourning the death of players who only exist on pieces of paper and who only act in response to the roll of dice, or deciding how many runs the Canada Moist Talkers should get when a base runner splits in two and both halves of him score, metafandom provides an outlet, and often a community, around sports, which can and often does exist independent of sports themselves. A world of sports involvement that in many ways can serve as a substitute for when the teams and leagues that traditionally draw our attention bore us, let us down, take advantage of us, or demand, through their actions, that we keep our distance.

I loved that old Lipton World Series poster so much that, a few years ago, I found a copy of it on eBay. I bought it, framed it, and had it mounted on the wall above the desk at which I'm typing this. I still look at it all the time. Sometimes, when I'm feeling burnt out about baseball and don't feel like watching it or writing about it, I'll close my eyes and see if I can still recite, in order, the matchups of every World Series going back to 1903. Sometimes I'll grab a few of the thousands of old baseball cards from my childhood that I still have in a closet, look at them, sort them, and put them away. Sometimes I'll break out my old Commodore 64 and play a few games of Accolade's

HardBall! game, which features the "All-Stars" vs. the "Champs" and colorfully named but entirely fictitious players such as Pepi Pérez and Guy José. I usually play as the All-Stars. I win most of the time.

When I do these things, I still feel engaged as a fan. It's just felt on a more personal, idiosyncratic level. A level that does not require me to think about the excesses of the sports-industrial complex, which often make sports difficult to watch and to support.

My fandom belongs to me. Not them. I can pursue it any way I want to. And so can you.

EPILOGUE

I have never been a soccer fan of any kind, really. I didn't play when I was a kid. I didn't follow international soccer when it became a somewhat trendy thing for people to do in the early 1990s once it became intermittently available in the US. And despite the fact that Columbus got one of the inaugural clubs, I didn't pay much attention to Major League Soccer when it began in 1996. The most I'd do is watch a couple of World Cup matches every four years, but I only did that because a lot of my friends were into it and I wanted to be able to talk about it with them. I enjoyed the World Cup matches and occasionally got into the drama of the tournament while it lasted, but I'd let go of all of it once it was over. I had enough sports in my life, I thought. Being a serious sports fan takes a lot of energy, and I had neither the free time nor the brain capacity to devote to becoming a proper fan of another one.

One Sunday afternoon last July, I was scrolling social media when I came across a couple of tweets from a friend who was getting ready to watch the UEFA Euro soccer final between England and Italy. I was bored and wasn't particularly interested in turning a baseball game on, so I decided to tune in to the match. It wasn't quite the World Cup, but it had the same vibe, so I decided to spend a couple of hours with it. And, despite the fact that I only had the vaguest idea of what was going on in the match beyond the basics, I really enjoyed it. While I never bothered to get into soccer, aesthetically speaking, I had always found the game to be exciting and pleasing. There's a satisfying geometry to it all that makes the other advance-on-the-goal/defend-the-goal games, like basketball, hockey, and even American football, pale in comparison. Maybe it's the size of the field and the open spaces? Maybe it's greater fluidity? I don't know, but there's a nice combination of order and chaos to the overall proceedings in soccer that scratches various itches I have that the other sports stopped scratching a long time ago. The England-Italy match scratched them, even though England—the team I decided to root for based on my shallow-but-undeniable Anglophilia—lost the match.

After the match, I asked myself why, if I enjoyed soccer so much, I didn't watch more of it. The only answers I could come up with were rooted in my old ideas about fandom. I didn't have a personal or historical connection to any soccer teams. Given my massive ignorance about the sport and its history, I couldn't call myself a *real* fan. How could I dive into soccer with the level of obsession I have for baseball and used to have for Ohio State Buckeyes games?

Since everything I've talked about in this book was squarely at the front of my mind last July—indeed, I had already submitted the first draft—I quickly realized the silliness of these reasons. I laughed to myself and realized that not only was there nothing stopping me from simply watching soccer, but that doing so, despite my ignorance and less-than-obsessive commitment to it, could serve as a pretty decent proof of concept for the entire enterprise. So I decided that, at least for the 2021–22 season, I'd get into English soccer and see where it took me.

The Premier League and other English leagues began in mid-August. As I write this, I have been watching multiple matches each weekend for about two months. So far, it's been exciting and entertaining, though not surprisingly, it's been a tad confusing at times as well.

As mentioned, I don't have decades' worth of knowledge, history, and storylines at my disposal like I do for American sports. So as I watched my first few matches, I spent a lot of time googling stuff like "what is offsides?" and "why does Tottenham hate Arsenal?" But though I lacked context, I was also free of decades' worth of predispositions, annoyances, and grudges floating around in my head. I didn't, like I do with American sports, find myself constantly thinking about what I *should be* thinking as the matches unfolded. I didn't feel obligated to analyze things or have strong opinions or some broader take about everything I saw.

I can't remember the last time I've watched a sporting event of almost any kind without it either engaging my passions or my critical thinking skills in a serious way, but watching soccer, at least so far, has been an experience in pure immersive recreation. An experience in letting go and giving myself over to the action and the atmosphere for the action and atmosphere's sake. The aesthetics for the aesthetics' sake. Learning as I go and forming impressions and, eventually, opinions of my own, but not opinions I have to have as part of some larger . . . thing into which so much else is tied. It's an experience I have not had with respect to any sport since I was a child, and the experience has been every bit as refreshing as it has been exciting.

Another thing I didn't have going into all of this was a rooting interest. Since English soccer became more available in the US, it's become something of a cliché for Americans to talk about some grand process they went through to choose which club to support. I've heard every possible justification you can imagine. As is the case in every sport, a lot of people are drawn to whoever happens to be good when they are introduced to the sport. In English soccer, that typically means one of the "Big Six" clubs: Manchester United, Manchester City, Chelsea, Liverpool, Arsenal, or Tottenham. If you have any English ancestry, you might go with a club from the place your great-great-grandparents came from. In the 1990s, I had one friend who chose Manchester City because he was a fan of Oasis and the Gallagher brothers supported them. I had another friend who chose Chelsea because that's who Damon Albarn of Blur backs. It's all over the map. The only common denominator I've found among my soccer-watching friends is that once a rooting interest is identified, their fan identity becomes nearly indistinguishable from that of a Reds fan from Cincinnati or a Tigers fan from Detroit. It's immutable. It just *is*.

At first, I began thinking along those lines myself. Three or four of my favorite bands of all time come from Manchester, so maybe I should root for City or United? My great-grandmother was from West Bromwich, so perhaps I should root for Albion? The manager of Liverpool is a big lefty like me, so maybe I should Up the Reds? Because of the World Cup and that Euro final, I've seen Tottenham's striker Harry Kane a few times, so maybe I should go all-in with the Spurs? But then I realized: I don't have to root for anyone. At least not for some contrived reason, born out by no more logic than the geography of one's birth that normally determines such things. I could just watch games, enjoy games, and if any sort of affinity for a given club forms, well, so be it. And that's what I've done.

In the early going, I've let my rooting interests remain fluid. In the first couple weeks of the season, I'd typically choose who I'd like to see win moments before or even after kickoff based on factors ranging from the color of a club's kits to the songs sung by the home crowd to whatever interesting storylines happened to be surrounding the club in the days leading up to the match. As the weeks wore on and my understanding of the game and the league grew, more sophisticated insights led the way, such as the emergence of a young player with promise or a particular style of play—aggressive or conservative—I found to be aesthetically pleasing. Some things turned me off, too, such as simply poor or uninspiring play. Through all of this so far, I have felt no obligation to pick a club to support simply to have a single club to support.

My fandom has been a very in-the-moment, fair-weather sort of thing. That lack of an all-in investment has meant that while no win has brought with it too much in the way of exuberance, no loss has upset me for more than a few fleeting moments, and that has felt positively liberating. I may eventually gravitate to a particular club, but if I do it, I'll do it for reasons that make some sense to me as opposed to having it foisted upon me by an accident of birth or an accident of geography. It's also worth noting that not tying myself to one club allows me to get a better handle on the business of the game and the nature of the men and corporate entities that own the various clubs. As is the case with bigtime sports everywhere, a great many of them are run by ethically dubious folks whose values and interests conflict with my own. By not deciding, arbitrarily, to go all-in with Manchester City, for example, I need not reconcile that fandom with the fact that the club is owned and controlled by members of a repressive authoritarian regime in Abu Dhabi. Maybe it's folly to expect anyone who is rich enough to own a major sports franchise to be on the side of the angels, but I feel at least a tad better by not committing myself to one of them so completely that I'll buy their merchandise and serve as a walking billboard for them or otherwise allow them to leverage my loyalty.

Not tying myself to a particular club has also meant that I've been able to watch many more of them play than

I would have had I made a point to catch every Tottenham or Manchester City or Everton match. As a result, I've seen players that, were I following a given club, would have taken me all season to see and appreciate. Guys like Adama Traoré of Wolverhampton. He's a huge man, seemingly chiseled from stone, who looks absolutely amazing on the pitch until the moment he has to shoot, at which point he looks lost. I don't know that I'd watch any Wolverhampton matches in the normal course, but I've made a point to check out some to see if Traoré has any better luck finishing this week than last. I'm kind of invested in him at this point. I'm likewise invested in Spurs forward Son Heung-min, who had some excellent matches early in the season when forced to carry a heavier load than normal due to Tottenham star Harry Kane sitting out for a couple of weeks. Kane, too, for that matter, is interesting to me. He's probably the most famous English soccer player at the moment, and one of sport's biggest stars, but in the early part of the season, there was drama surrounding his reported desire to leave Tottenham and be transferred to Manchester City. If I were a Spurs fan, I suppose this might sour me on him. If I were a City fan, it might make me covet him. If I were a fan of one of their rivals, perhaps that would cause me any number of feelings as well. In the event, though, I kind of don't care. I'll watch him play wherever, enjoy his game for its own sake, and watch with genuine interest—instead of some disdain or fervor born of team loyalty—to see how he does in his new setting. Or, if he stays with the Spurs, his old one.

One of the reasons the Euros final last July stuck with me to the point where I wanted to stick with soccer was something that happened after the match. The match ended with Italy beating England on penalty kicks. During the shutout, English players Bukayo Saka, Marcus Rashford, and Jadon Sancho—all of whom are Black—missed their kicks. In the aftermath, they received horrific racist abuse on social media from English fans. Racism in English and European soccer is not at all a new phenomenon, but now more than ever, those involved with the game and those who report on it are making an effort to talk openly about it and, at least to some extent, own up to it in ways they never have before.

Racism in soccer is obviously a massive and deep-rooted issue that will take a long time to solve, but in the meantime, it has given socially conscious fans a reason to root for Saka, even if they don't root for Arsenal; to root for Rashford and Sancho, even if they don't root for Manchester United; and to back the voices around the league such as Liverpool manager Jürgen Klopp, Aston Villa defender Tyrone Mings, and others who have, at no small risk to their popularity and marketability, spoken out against their own club's supporters and against political figures who have engaged in unseemly behavior or retrograde public commentary about race and activism in the game.

Finally, I have gotten all kinds of enjoyment from soccer on the level of metafandom and by simple virtue of being around the sport and some of its fans.

On the opening weekend of the Premier League season, I went to a pub that opens up at 7:00 a.m. and shows English soccer matches all day long. There, I met a Manchester United fan who was there for the team's early match against Leeds, a Chelsea fan who had accompanied him, and a Leicester fan who was there for no particular reason. All of them pitched their rooting interests to me, complete with references to club lore, club history (both honorable and dubious), club traditions, and the like. One guy there was not a fan of any Premier League club. Rather, he was a fan of Peterborough, which competes in English football's second tier. He had called ahead to get one of the pub's TVs set to Peterborough's match against Derby County just for him. The Peterborough fan and I talked for an hour about how and why Americans get into English soccer, about how he fell in with Peterborough, and about all of the other silly aspects of trying to follow a sport with which one has no organic connection, be it geography, family history, or what have you, from across an ocean. As we talked, he bought me a beer. Later, I picked up the bill for his breakfast. As the Peterborough match ended and we got ready to leave, he gave me his Peterborough scarf as a souvenir of my first day as an English soccer fan—and, he said, as a not-so-subtle push to get me to support Peterborough going forward. If I do so, that'll likely make two of us in all of Ohio. You find your community where you can.

Even if I'm declining to go all-in with a rooting interest at the moment, I found simply being around people who were excited about their sport to be a delightful experience. I have found the jargon and figures of speech surrounding English football to be both charming and enlightening (whereas hyperbole is the order of the day when it comes to American sports commentary, dry understatement is the go-to for English announcers). My Anglophilic side is likewise satisfied by having an excuse to look up English towns and bits of English history with which I am unfamiliar. So much of what I have enjoyed about soccer so far has actually had very little to do with the soccer itself as opposed to the stuff that orbits it.

It may be unconventional to root for every club a little bit and no club a lot. It may be unusual to be a fan of individual players, even rivals, no matter where they play. For those who see sports as an escape from the real world, it may be anathema to take a great interest in how sports figures are grappling with real world problems. For some people, it may seem silly to be just as invested in the somewhat superfluous things that surround sports as you are in the sports themselves. That's how I'm doing it, though. And despite decades of loyalty-based, rah-rah sports fandom, it was not particularly hard to make the switch.

All it took was a little rethinking.

ACKNOWLEDGEMENTS

I would like to thank Anne Trubek for seeing the potential in a book about sports that will inevitably piss off a lot of sports fans. There are probably more effective ways of setting money on fire than telling people that they are wrong about a thing they love, but at the moment I'm struggling to think of any. That Anne thinks differently about it is a credit to either her savvy or her sense of humor, both of which are considerable. Without Anne's faith, mentorship, and guidance this book would never have seen the light of day.

Thanks to Dan Crissman and Michael Jauchen whose editorial suggestions, copyediting and proofing helped turn an unhinged manifesto into a far, far better-written unhinged manifesto. Thanks to David Wilson who created the wonderful cover of this book and to Phoebe Mogharei who handled publicity. Thanks as well to fellow Belt Publishing author Elizabeth Catte, who hipped me to what writing for Belt was all about and helped me to understand how well its way of doing things suited my habits and temperament as a writer. You were absolutely right about that, Elizabeth.

Special thanks is owed to my oldest and dearest friend, Ethan Stock. Ethan has been editing my work since Freshman year English class at Ohio State in 1991 and, my God, that's not easy work. Ethan took it upon himself to do a separate, preliminary copyedit of his own which, in many ways, was like cleaning one's house before the housekeeper arrives, but boy howdy it was necessary. By virtue of Ethan's work several editorial train wrecks were averted there are now considerably fewer sentence fragments and misplaced hyphens in this book than there might've been, even if I kept a whole hell of a lot more of them in there than Ethan wanted me to.

Thanks also to my second-oldest and equally dear friend Megan Kindle who spent years urging me to write a book despite me offering all manner of excuses for why I shouldn't or couldn't. Writers spend a lot of time doubting themselves. Having a friend who won't let you do that is essential, and I am struggling to think of a friend who has greater confidence in me than Megan.

Most of the ideas in this book would either be half-baked at best or things I never considered at all if it were not for other writers, thinkers, and commentators who have covered a good bit of this ground in the past and with whom I have discussed it all over the years. This includes my former NBC colleagues Bill Baer, Aaron Gleeman, Matthew Pouliot, D.J.

Short, Drew Silva, Ashley Varela, and Nick Stellini, who put up with my often insufferable tumbthumping about the sports industrial complex but nonetheless inspired me to rant and rave even more. It also includes J.C. Bradbury, Howard Bryant, Keith Law, Rob Neyer, Brian Alexander, Mike Duncan, Kavitha Davidson, Jessica Luther, Nelson Schwartz, Shakeia Taylor, Steven Goldman, Tova Wang, Lincoln Mitchell, Frank Guridy, Adrian Burgos Jr., Marc Normandin, Neil deMause, Luis Schiff, Robert Jarvis, Joe Sheehan, Eugene Freedman, Ruth Kapelus, Laura Wagner, Claire McNear, John Thorn, Sheryl Ring, Jay Jaffe, Katie Strang, Britt Ghiroli, Bradford William Davis, Hannah Keyser, Lindsey Adler, Emma Baccellieri, Jen Mac Ramos, Stacy Mae Fowles, Craig Edwards, Jesse Spector, Grant Brisbee, Mike Ferrin, Liz Roscher, and Britni de la Cretaz. I am certain I have inadvertently left many others who were critical to the development of my thinking as a writer off this list, and for that I apologize.

I would also like to acknowledge and thank the subscribers to my newsletter, Cup of Coffee, and those who have read me at the various others places I have written over the years. who quite literally support me, financially speaking, but who likewise give me fantastic, often critical feedback and who provide no shortage of inspiration.

Most importantly, I would like to thank my family.

Thanks to my wife, Allison Calcaterra who serves as my first, second, third and fourth-through one millionth source of emotional support. Allison understands that even though writing requires hours upon hours hunched over in front of a computer screen, sometimes it's best to get up, get a drink of water, and maybe go for a walk.

Thanks to my children, Anna and Carlo, for constantly reminding me why I do what I do while also reminding me that I'm nowhere near as clever as I sometimes think I am. That's way more useful than you might think.

Thank you to my brother Curtis Calcaterra for sharing his love of baseball card collecting with me which did more than anything to make me into a sports fan.

Finally, thanks to my parents, Richard and Lezlie Calcaterra who, even if they are not particularly big sports fans themselves, encouraged my love of sports as a kid while making sure I never got too high or too low because of something I or someone else did on a baseball diamond, a football field, a basketball court, or a bowling alley. This book could would not exist if I didn't love sports, but it likewise would not exist if wasn't taught about what's truly important in life.

CPSIA information can be obtained
at www.ICGtesting.com
Printed in the USA
JSHW030757040222
22504JS00005B/6